KABBALAH AND CONSCIOUSNESS

AND THE POETRY OF

ALLEN AFTERMAN

KABBALAH AND CONSCIOUSNESS

AND THE POETRY OF

ALLEN AFTERMAN

THE SHEEP MEADOW PRESS

RIVERDALE-ON-HUDSON, NEW YORK

All inquiries and permission requests should be addressed to:
  The Sheep Meadow Press
  P. O. Box 1345
  Riverdale-on-Hudson, NY 10471

Designed and typeset by The Sheep Meadow Press.
Distributed by The University Press of New England.

Library of Congress Cataloging-in-Publication Data

Afterman, Allen B.
 Kabbalah and consciousness and the poetry of Allen Afterman.
  p. cm.
 Includes four books of poetry by the author: Desire for white, Maze rose, Purple Adam, and In the other.
 ISBN 1-931357-23-4 (alk. paper)
 1. Cabala--History. 2. Mysticism--Judaism. I. Title.

BM526.A36 2005
296.1'6--dc22

2005000793

TABLE OF CONTENTS

For Susan

A POET'S KABBALAH
(A CRITICAL NOTE BY RODGER KAMENETZ)

I never had the chance to meet Allen Afterman before his untimely death, except through his poetry and prose, but I have long felt very grateful to him and his work. When I first began to look into kabbalah fifteen years ago, I searched in vain for a felt connection to the maddeningly abstruse material. After all, this was Jewish mysticism, which I felt somehow belonged to me, yet the formulations, while intriguing, were also baffling. In the scholarly books, I detected the light, but only dimly filtered through a maze of footnotes and dense argumentation. But when I opened *Kabbalah and Consciousness*, I found a language that went straight to the heart. And in the poems that join it, I found something more: a contemporary poet writing in the spirit of the psalms.

Poets are often iconoclastic, myth-shatterers as much as myth makers. Many poets are therefore skeptical of a religiously-based system like kabbalah—one famous Israeli poet warned me away from taking kabbalah classes in Jerusalem. To him kabbalah was "bad poetry." He had been raised in an orthodox tradition and his path led him to rebel against it.

However, Allen Afterman's path moved in the opposite direction. Having already lived many gilgulim—incarnations: distinguished lawyer and legal scholar in the United States, and a sheep rancher in Australia—Allen Afterman came to kabbalah and to Israel in 1981 as the culmination of a personal spiritual journey. As a seeker and a student, he did not attempt to remake kabbalah for our time—which has been the bold project, for instance, of the Jewish renewal movement. Instead, he accepted the tradition as taught by a traditional teacher, Rabbi Yitzhak Ginsburgh.

The effort to find the best language for what cannot be said goes on and always will. Kabbalah writes a major chapter in that effort, one with peculiar resonance in our troubled time for Jews and non-Jews alike. Yet, unlike other attractive forms of mysticism promoted in what can unfortunately be described as a spiritual supermarket—if not fast food chain—Jewish mysticism by its nature eschews the personal. This is part of the challenge Afterman faces. *Kabbalah and Consciousness* was intended, writes its author, as an introduction to kabbalah for "the general reader." What is the "general reader," whoever he or she may be, to make of the terse intricate complex inner universe of kabbalah? Deeply rooted in Jewish text—Torah and Talmud are its ground—its language can seem arcane to those unfamiliar with those texts. Its insights are often expressed in diagram and schema, such as the chart of the ten *sefirot* discussed in Chapter VI. At first glance, these charts of the intricate intrapersonal relationships of the One can seem baffling—wiring diagrams of unknown realms of existence. They can feel remote.

But Afterman has given us a kabbalah for poets, not in the sense of "physics for poets"—some slack version of a complex system, but rather a kabbalah written into fresh contemporary language—a kabbalah alive to the core difficulty of language and image—a difficulty that every poet wrestles with, but few with the kind of spiritual seriousness Allen Afterman brings to bear.

That's clear from the selection of poems from *Desire for White* that culminates and fulfills the first part of the book, a selection whose power cannot be counted in pages. The prose and the poetry need to be read together for they both struggle in language and against language to do the impossible. Kabbalah attempts to capture the infinite in finite thought and words. The "desire for white" is the impossible desire to know God intimately. To receive, in the image that concludes the poems, "the white kisses of your mouth."

The echo of the *Song of Songs* is deliberate. The Jewish tradition has long interpreted these love lyrics in a mystical sense as an allegory of the soul's longing for God. But the typically chaste and simple diction of this line reflect not only a modernist poetic sensibility, but an intensity that seals Afterman's poetry and prose.

This intensity comes not only from his personal spiritual struggle but also arises from the poet's specific struggle with language. As a poet, Afterman knows very well what kabbalah asserts in a very bold trope: that the world of matter is itself composed of images.

Not to say that the world is completely illusory as Eastern traditions hold—*samsara* or *Maya*. But rather that, as Afterman writes, "There is an eternal dimension in every aspect of reality. A 'spark of the light or Infinity' is captured in each of the forms or images which constitute the everyday world: that is, these images are enlivened by its energy. The 'images suck' on the life force of Infinite Light while at the same time, they block awareness of its existence."

Here we have the paradox that the very images that come to us, whether "out there," or "in here," threaten to conceal what they reveal—their source in the infinite One. Images and words are shells, opaque and empty at once:

"The shell
is form—

is the dome
is the skull

—is the density of nothingness,"

At the most, in our yearning, we can taste an absence, a disappearance; we can make choices "between losses." Our images are inadequate, our language shattered. The Jewish mystics say, "the world is wrong names"—and at the same time, the world of wrong names is where the poet begins to work, it is the only world we have. The "Desire for White"—the desire for God, is an impossibility that is also our obliteration. White is both the consummation and obliteration of all light—yet we live, as the poet says in his poems, perpetually on the other side, even while affirming that "From your side" —God's side—"light doesn't die." And the yearning is painful; in his desire for white, "the eyelids are cut from my eyes."

God has many names in Jewish mystical thought, but the most intimate, the one Afterman chooses in his poetry, is "you." Not even you with a capital 'y', but the you we desire to be in intimacy with and familiar to.

Another favorite metaphor for God in the kabbalah—is light. God as God is in God's self—is white light, but for the poet—

"my mouth

is the
prism"
—meaning that necessarily, we as finite creatures, using words and images, can only separate out colors from that unity, "forms of light/ tiny screams like isolated stars."

The shattering of the vessels is necessary for there to have been creation at all, so teaches the Lurianic kabbalah. Chassidism translated that cosmology into a psychology. "The fall of Adam," Afterman writes, "symbolizes the shattering of the primordial unity of human consciousness. The 'shattered' nature of ordinary consciousness parallels the primordial cosmic cataclysm known as the Breaking of the Vessels" (6).

Idolatry then is not only a spiritual problem; it is a problem in how we relate to the images in our minds. "Idolizing" means mistaking the part for the whole—in Hebrew the word idol, "pessel," means a fragment or broken piece. In pursuing fragments and pieces of the divine light, we become confused, unable to "control the chaos of...thoughts and emotions." We split the world into halves, good and evil, right and wrong, male and female, spiritual and physical, or we fall pray to the various ideologies and -isms that hold up one side of the split against the other: nationalism, materialism, egoism. The devotion that ought to go only to the One is given instead to the fragment.

The kabbalist seeks a vision of the whole, but only to return to the broken world—and make repairs. Rabbi Isaac Luria's kabbalah first articulated this great drama: not only the drama of the shattering of the vessels but also the "tikkun olam" or healing of the world. Luria found these dramas encoded in the Torah, and also in Jewish history. They are eternal moments outside of ordinary time, that imprint time with their pattern. These two eternal cosmic moments mark themselves in the fall of man and the hope-for redemption in the messianic age, but they mark themselves also in every human life and moment. The shattering is reflected in our personal despair and alienation, the tikkun in every renewed effort we make to heal in our hope and yearning for the light. In that sense the teachings of kabbalah promise the possibility of making every moment in our lives meaningful.

The poet too, working with images, seeks to reveal the

white light they conceal, that is the primordial task and difficulty of poetry. The shattering and tikkun are a cycle of the creative process: the poet sees the light, but the words conceal it. Even the very same poem, read at different times, may at one time open the heart, and another time seem opaque, dead stone. But as a kabbalist, Afterman asserts that solid rock and stone, are themselves "images;" our broken seeing fails to see the light they "suck" on. "The struggle of consciousness is to liberate itself through the reunification of... images." Poetry struggles with this task as well.

In Chapter VI, Afterman describes the mind of the spiritually advanced person, the "tzaddik"—literally the righteous one—who has reached the level of constantly practicing the commandments (mitzvahs) of consciousness. Traditionally there are 613 mitzvot or commandments read in the Torah, and they govern everything from moral behavior, to ritual, to cuisine. However, among these are seven mitzvahs that primarily govern consciousness—they are concerned with where attention is focused from moment to moment. We could say these are purely inward directed mitzvahs, except that in fact in Jewish thought, the mystic is rarely seen as a solitary spiritual athlete. His duty—the "her" is not mentioned in this context by Afterman or his teachers—is to help others find the connection with the divine. For the "hasid" the rebbe or beloved teacher is the tzaddik.

We "general readers" are clearly not tzaddikim, nor is the author, but the tzaddik's mind is a model, a template. The tzaddik's struggle with lust, with ego, with depression, even with madness, are our struggles as well. By analogy, we also detect here the poet's seriousness, the ferocity of the poet's struggle with images, when Afterman writes, "The battle for the mind is for the content of its imagery; it is the battle for the person himself, who is where his mind is" (p. 61).

For Afterman kabbalah is primarily a poetic psychology, as well as a psychological poetics. Creation, the Garden of Eden, the fall—take place in the consciousness of each individual. The term that mediates kabbalah and consciousness is the image. And that is a poetic term of course as well. Ordinarily we distinguish between images "out there"—the images the objective world presents us, such as rocks, trees or flowers—and the images "in here," the images in dreams or that arise through creative work, and that for the poet to find their expression in words. But for the kabbalist, there is no such distinction: the universe is "holographic"— Afterman seems to have borrowed the term from the freelance philosopher Ken Wilber—that is, at each scale of consideration it repeats the pattern of the highest scale. The processes of the psyche are the poetics of the universe. "Human consciousness is the analogue of, and is isomorphically the same as, all the levels of existence" (p.7).

If I have highlighted the poetics of Afterman's presentation it is in part because he reveals himself only indirectly. Because of Jewish mystical tradition, because of the complex nature of the subject, the presentation of kabbalah can be very heady, intellectual and impersonal. There are very few works of mystical spiritual autobiography in the Jewish tradition. Instead, we can get at most hints. Afterman does not exactly open up his life to clear inspection in these pages, but glimpses of a real human being struggling with real feelings refreshes them. And anyone can see by reading the poetry, that many of the images that arise in the prose find their counterpart in the verse. Apart from poetry, a second locus where Afterman's passion intersects kabbalah is in his personal life decision to immigrate and raise a family in the land of Israel. His Chapter VIII is an extraordinary prose poem about the difficulties of that ecstatic tortured land, and his words, if anything, read even truer today than they do when they were first written more than twenty years ago. The writing is searing and Afterman is a seer. If any reader wants to understand the passion and even the madness that might draw a Jewish soul to leave Exile and struggle in the unpromising uncompromising promised land, this passage would serve as a heartfelt manifesto. At the same time, we cannot help but be aware in our own time of the dangers of such a heady brew of mysticism and nationalism.

In the end, Afterman is always a poet, in the poetry of course but also in the sudden flashes of illumination and brilliant formulations in the prose, that jump off the wiring diagram like living sparks. Though he addresses consciousness in general, his prose reflects a poetic consciousness—and this is unique in our time. Other authors have given us the kabbalah of scholars or the kabbalah of rabbis, but this is the kabbalah of a poet.

—Rodger Kamenetz

AFTERWORD

My father, Allen Afterman, died suddenly in Jerusalem on December 14, 1992. He was 51 years old. Now, more than a decade later, I wish to present a few points about Allen and his writing that may be relevant to the readers of this book.

In several of his poems, Allen uses the spiral as an image of growth, of evolution and intensification of life. Similarly, his own life can be seen as opening in spiral movement, spanning through different continents, different spiritual modes and activities.

He was born in Los Angeles on May 21, 1941. His parents, Russian Jewish migrants, had arrived in the U.S.A. as children. He studied at U.C.L.A. and Harvard Law School, successfully completing a graduate Law degree. Later, he took a position as Lecturer in Law at the University of Auckland, New Zealand, as one of his professors had recommended New Zealand as an exotic place to visit. From there he moved to Australia, teaching law at the University of Melbourne, and completing a Master of Law degree, his thesis for which was published as the book: *Company Directors and Controllers* (1970), still a standard text book in Australian universities. Another book, *Cases And Materials; Corporations And Associations*, written jointly with Robert Baxt, was published in 1973. During this period he taught Contract Law and Corporate Law, in various Universities in Australia, Singapore, and New Zealand.

In 1972, faced with the option of a post as the youngest Professor of Law at that time in Australia, he decided to retire from academic life and to devote himself to writing poetry. He subsequently moved to a farm in southern New South Wales with my mother, Susan, and published two books of poetry, *The Maze Rose* (1974), and *Purple Adam* (1980). During this period he also learned many physical skills associated with farming and living on the land.

In 1980, after eight years of life in the bush, they moved on again, this time to Israel. The decision to immigrate to Israel was taken while living there for a year in 1978. In Israel, as in Australia, my parents chose to live on the land. They managed, together with a couple of friends, to buy private land in the Western Galilee, to plant olive groves, and to take part in the establishment of a beautiful place, now the successful community called Clil.

While living in Clil, Allen published two books with The Sheep Meadow Press: *Desire for White* (1991), a book of poems that combined both new and previously published work; and *Kabbalah and Consciousness* (1992), an effort to express his personal mystical world within the kabbalistic framework. These two projects were connected, and were different manifestations of his life and experience.

We who were close to him had the opportunity to experience this life and creativity in other dimensions: in his singing, in the stone walls and terraces that he built on the farm, in the taste of his olive oil.

Both the poems and the book on Kabbalah were influeced by certain personal mystical experiences. His relation with these experiences was paradoxical. On the one hand he did not seek to develop or repeat them through regular meditation- related exercises or other forms of seeking. On the other hand, he developed a tenacious and intense loyalty to them, working the exact movement that he had experienced over and over in his mind, and in his writings. Many of the experiences and insights articulated in his poetry were derived from his singing. Allen was a Gypsy singer, like his mother, whom he learned from and performed with prior to her death. Another medium of creativity and receptivity for him was the desert, where he would take long solitary walks.

An important aspect of his spiritual activity was his individual approach. Although he sensed very much that he was part of the ancient Jewish spiritual tradition, and was specially connected to Hassidism, he was not part of any religious group or institution.

Allen studied Torah and Kabbalah with several people over the years, especially with my mother and close friends (as he acknowledges in his preface to *Kabbalah and Consciousness*). He acknowledged as well, the special dialogue he had over a six-year period with the Kabbalist Rav. Y. Ginzburgh. The manner in which Rav. Ginsburgh chose to learn with him is unique. Instead of reading classic Kabbalistic texts, he used Allen's poems and experiences as a starting point that allowed them to indulge in a verbal meditation of Kabbalistic material (these sessions were taped). It should be noted, however, that despite their unique connection, they had substantial disputes regarding political issues and the value of Humanistic and Universal values. Allen's sudden death preempted a book that he had begun writing, whose intention was to present and articulate from within the Jewish mystical sources a humanistic and universal view of the role of Israel, in it's relation with other nations.

I wish to thank our friend Stanley Moss for his genuine friendship and commitment to my father's memory and work. A reading of both earlier and later (and until now unpublished) poems, which have been included in this edition of *Kabbalah and Consciousness and Collected Poetry*, will, I hope, add depth and help reveal the personal journey of a special man.

—Adam Afterman

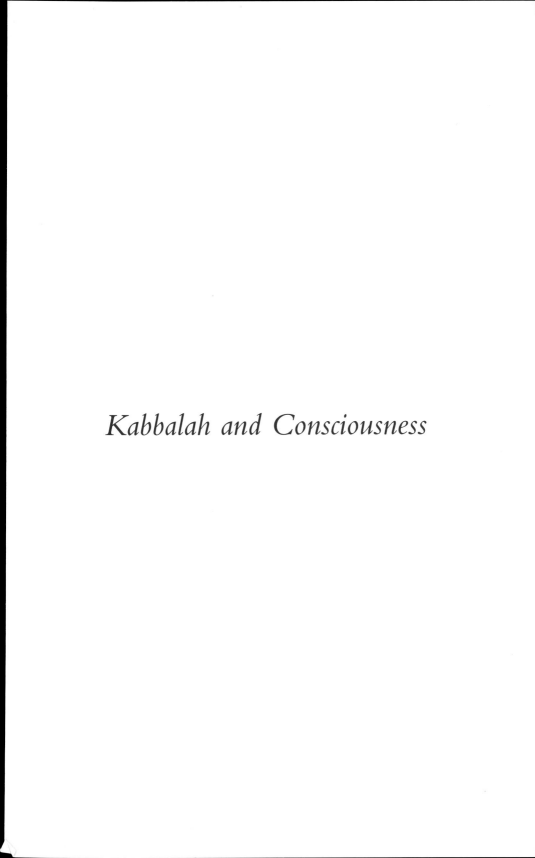

Kabbalah and Consciousness

AUTHOR'S PREFACE

Kabbalah, the mystical level of Torah interpretation, was reserved in the past for a spiritual elite who had mastered Torah and Talmudic study. Without such a background, it is virtually impossible to understand the classic books of Kabbalah such as the *Zohar* or the works of Rabbi Isaac Luria of Safed (known as the Holy *Ari*). The knowledge of Kabbalah was confined to elite circles of kabbalists, and was passed from master to disciple through the generations. Even today it is not taught in most *yeshivot* (seminaries). The intention in writing *Kabbalah and Consciousness* was to enable the general reader with no specific background in Judaism or Kabbalah to gain an insight into the inner life of the Jewish mystical tradition. The emphasis therefore is upon *experience*, and upon the relevance and impact of the ideas and processes of Kabbalah upon consciousness. The major theme in this work is that of ascent: the movement from ordinary consciousness to knowledge of and union with the Infinite. The second major theme in this work is that of the rectification of reality (*tikkun*): the process by which the eternal is revealed in all manifestations of everyday reality. Within the context of these movements, a major concern is the exploration of male and female modes of being.

The approach taken in this work follows that of most books of Kabbalah which tend to develop and intensify in accord with the logic of analogy rather than that of systematic exposition. The compacted style is also traditional. The work does not compare the Jewish mystical tradition with other traditions, nor does it defend or critically analyze the ideas of Kabbalah from a philosophical or historical perspective. The attempt has been to present kabbalistic concepts at a reasonable level of depth while not drawing the reader too far into the complexities. Nevertheless, the more background the reader brings, the more he may appreciate a new approach, expression, and in some cases, interpretation of otherwise known themes. Extensive footnotes have been used to provide a second level of commentary as well as to cite sources. Upon the initial reading, therefore, the reader may wish to pass over the footnotes so as not to be distracted from the primary voice and movement.

The last Chapter, entitled *An Overview of the Kabbalistic Reality*, presents a general survey of the main themes and structure of kabbalistic thought. Some of the material is discussed in more depth than is perhaps strictly necessary to elucidate the main text. Nevertheless, it is useful for the reader to have before him an idea of the larger framework of ideas and structure in which the main body of the text takes place. Those readers who are not familiar with the main concepts of Kabbalah may wish to first read the Overview. *Desire for White* is a poem written during the same period as this work which explores many of the themes considered in the main text. As with the Overview, some readers may prefer to begin with the poem. Either of these options is logical from the standpoint of the work itself.

—Allen Afterman

ACKNOWLEDGEMENTS

Kabbalah and Consciousness developed from a personal dialogue over a six-year period between the author and the well-known kabbalist and teacher, Rav Y. Ginsburgh. The final version has taken its own path but these meetings are at its core. I would therefore like to acknowledge my profound debt to Rav Ginsburgh in respect to the unique opportunity that I was given to learn Kabbalah from a kabbalist of his stature, and for his many re-readings of the manuscript. The responsibility for the views expressed however, is that of the author.

I would also like to thank Rav G. Fleer, whose careful readings and criticism of the work yielded many important insights and improvements. I owe a debt for the contribution of my friend and *havruta*, A. Goldman, with whom I explored new aspects and applications of kabbalistic thinking. As well, my thanks to Rabbi M. Odenheimer for insights and helpful suggestions. Thanks are due to Marc Radzyner who undertook the demanding task of transcribing the original tapes. Finally, I would also like to acknowledge the contribution made by my wife Susan. Her insights and criticism to both the kabbalistic and literary dimensions are reflected in every aspect of this work.

Man is the creature created for the purpose of experiencing God…One must strive to remove every obstacle of evil [the power of concealment] inherent in the darkness of materiality, and of day to day life; and strive to bring oneself close to God, until one unifies with Him, and becomes complete in His perfection. This is all that God desires of man, and it is the entire purpose of his creation…

—Rabbi Moshe Chaim Luzzatto*

* Italian kabbalist, known as the RaMChal (1707-1746). *The Way of God* (Feldheim, 1981), pp. 45, 24

INTRODUCTION

Kabbalah expresses the holographic, poetic universe of Judaism. As much as it is philosophical it is even more a map of transcendent experience. As one begins to appreciate and internalize this knowledge, one's understanding is focused on the unity of all aspects of existence and on their one source in the infinite. Just as acts which reveal infinity liberate day-to-day life, the thought of infinity liberates ordinary consciousness. Jewish mystical consciousness can be understood as seeking to restore the state of pure being which existed before the fall of Adam. Messianic consciousness, its ultimate goal, begins in the Garden, and seeks the ultimate union.

According to the teachings of Kabbalah, reality is a composite of images produced by the play of the light of Infinity. Both human consciousness and the physical world result from the progressive screenings or "enclothements" of light into images. The purpose of such screenings is to allow the world to manifest and not be obliterated. Rocks, trees, the human body—all physical objects—are images or forms ("vessels") which themselves are made of "thickened" light: so opaque, however, that the inner "spark" of infinite life is concealed. From the human perspective, therefore, the mind sees only the image: the "Sinai mountains", a "beautiful woman". Just as Einstein has shown that matter is only a form of energy, the light of Infinity is both the life force or creative energy of the universe, and its only substance. The inner essence of this light is God's love.

God creates something from nothing, the finite from the infinite, the imperfect from the perfect. This something has only apparent and conditional existence. There is nothing other than God. Nevertheless, man's view and experience of the Creation is also true because God recreates the images of reality every moment *ex nihilo* to serve His purpose.

The question as to why God created the world cannot be answered satisfactorily by philosophy. Any answer constitutes a contradiction or a limitation of His perfection: He does not need the world, He has no desires, etc. The Cosmos is God's; He creates for His own purpose.[1] It is a

5

matter of Jewish belief, however, that this purpose is benevolent; that God's "passion is to dwell below", to give of Himself. God's purpose in creating the world and His love are the same. Although this level of God's "mind" remains paradoxical,[2] all report experiencing the unity and the absolute goodness of the Creation as they penetrate consciousness. Thus Judaism teaches that God created man for the purpose of experiencing the Infinite.

The fall of Adam symbolizes the shattering of the primordial unity of human consciousness. The "shattered" nature of ordinary consciousness parallels the primordial cosmic cataclysm known as the Breaking of the Vessels.[3] The cosmic Breaking of the Vessels, which is the genesis of reality, could be likened to the breakdown of the mind resulting from an overwhelming revelation or mystical experience. The mind is too immature a "vessel" to hold the pure revelation of the light of Infinity and cannot integrate it into its ordinary awareness. It breaks apart—that is, it begins to invest phenomena and people with god-like qualities, most especially the ego. It may run from one shining fragment to the next, idolizing each and then rejecting it. The mind may embrace visions, then become violent; it may run back and forth from one teaching to the next, fall in and out of love, in and out of fear.

The extent of the fall or breakage in each person's consciousness is expressed by the distance his awareness is from the infinite, and by the degree to which aspects or components of reality are idolized. In everyday life, this is experienced inwardly as a person's inability to control the chaos of his thoughts and emotions; or at times, as a profound although sometimes repressed sense of meaninglessness and futility. Outwardly, it is experienced as the drive towards possession and power in all of its manifestations.

There is an eternal dimension in every aspect of reality. A "spark" of the light of Infinity is "captured" in each of the forms or images which constitute the everyday world; that is, these images are enlivened by its energy. The images "suck" on the life force of infinite Light, while at the same time, they block awareness of its existence. Ordinary consciousness (the fall from the Garden of Eden) manifests primarily in the fundamental dualities of life and death, good and evil, spiritual and physical, etc., which break down further into the various modern forms of "idol worship" (e.g., egoism, materialism, nationalism, excessive categorization of knowledge and specialization, etc.). The struggle of consciousness is to liberate itself through the reunification of these images.

The procreative drive (and the emotion of love itself) is, at the most fundamental level, the drive to return to primordial unity, to divine nothingness (*ayin*).[4] (Gravity and the other attractive forces known by physics can be understood as manifesting the analogous drive in nature to return to its primordial singularity). Thus the process of rectification is that of unification. In order to achieve this unity, however, the mind struggles not only against its own fragmented structure but against its psychic and physical drives which are guided by imagination. The unrectified imagination seeks union with itself (fantasy or egoism), and with the various sources of physical or spiritual intensity which it encounters. The mind is constantly grasping at aspects of truth, or losing itself in partial or lower manifestations of unity. The very structure and analytic processes of the mind lead it towards idolatry.

The process of rectification (*tikkun*)[5] is the returning of mankind and all of physical nature into unity with God. In the Jewish view, therefore, it is impossible and also meaningless to pursue a private enlightenment. The ideal is not asceticism or monasticism but rather their opposite. Every person is obligated to try to marry, have children, make a living, and be part of the community. The Jewish approach is to rectify the mind and body by re-directing their forces and desires, not by their elimination. Although there is an ascetic tradition among the kabbalists, asceticism is considered constructive only to balance an overflowing soul. Worship or practice that is not based on joy is considered destructive. The essential path is that of praise: praise of God, praise of life, praise of man who is created in the image of God. This is the seemingly impossible spiritual task assumed by Judaism.

Kabbalah sees in man a microcosm of the universe; all levels of reality are therefore comprehensible except the nature of God Himself. Human consciousness is the analogue of, and is isomorphically the same as, all the levels of existence. This unity is expressed through the universal structure of the ten *sefirot*,[6] which is considered to be both the underlying structure of the universe, and the process by which reality is being created. Clarified consciousness "runs and returns" between the Infinite and ordinary levels of reality (from nothingness to somethingness, from somethingness to nothingness) like an angel ascending and descending the ladder in Jacob's dream. This ladder can be thought of as the *sefirot*.

Halachah (the "going" or way of Jewish law) is the body of commandments which structure and ritualize Jewish life in order to unify or uplift everyday reality to its source in the infinite. The commandments (*mitzvot*) connect ordinary acts such as eating, sex, work, etc. to the eternal); in this sense, they are "practical" physical acts of infinity. (The reincarnation of souls represents this process of rectification through the generations.) *Mitzvot*, practiced with the right intention (which ideally involves detachment from every desire for reward), lead towards ultimate knowledge and union.

NOTES

1. In the famous debate between the House of Hillel and the House of Shammai in the 1st century B.C.E., these two great schools of Torah interpretation differed in that the House of Shammai asserted that it would have been better for man had he not been created at all. [*Er. 13b.*] The debate was resolved in favor of the House of Shammai, principally because of the fear that man would not be successful in his effort to rectify the world.

2. Put in other terms, this paradox may be thought of as the internal "lining" or interface of the "womb" created by the *tzimtzum* within God's light. As a child living in that womb, a person cannot ordinarily penetrate it except in the experience of mystical union. See Overview, sect. 1: The Creation, and the *Tzimtzum*.

3. See Overview, sect. 4: The Breaking of the Vessels.

4. See Overview, sect. 1: The Creation, and the *Tzimtzum*.

5. See Overview, sect. 6: The Rectification of Reality (*Tikkun*).

6. See Overview, sect. 3: The Tree of Life (The Ten *Sefirot*); and sect. 2: The Five Worlds.

Chapter I

The Unity of Consciousness

1. Man as a Microcosm of Reality

Judaism seeks to unite man's eyes with God's eyes, that man see as much as is humanly possible as God sees. This is the essence of the rectification of consciousness (*tikkun*). To see with God's eyes, as it were, is possible because man is created in the image of God, and is himself a microcosm of reality. God's saying: "Let us make man in our image, after our likeness" [Gen. 1:26], can be interpreted to refer to the universe.[1] Man, made in the image of God, is created through the universe—which itself is alive and conscious. All of existence is one unity, one life. The elements and processes which form and sustain the Cosmos, sustain man. Within the human subconscious is the consciousness of stone, of trees, of all of the animals that have ever existed, of the sun, of the moon, of the spiral galaxies. Man's eyes are the eyes of the universe.

The structures of the body, the psyche, the soul, and the universe are considered analogues of each other (See Figures 7-9, Overview). This unity, in turn, is reflected in the structure of the commandments (*mitzvot*), the realm of physical action. The performance of each of the 613 *mitzvot* relate to the rectification of each of the 613 "limbs" or power centers of the body and of the soul, which in turn relate to their corresponding aspects of consciousness—and therefore to the ultimate rectification of reality.[2] The opportunity for each of the 600,000 archetypal souls of Israel to perform each of the 613 *mitzvot* is the messianic goal of the process of reincarnation.[3]

A major implication of the microcosmic and holographic structure of the psyche is that man subconsciously "knows" what his science is seeking to articulate. According to this understanding, intuitive insights, stimulated by rigorous scientific observation and inquiry, involve a process of "memory" or of meditative communion with the universe. It may be that the subconscious discovers by activating its innate experience with the universal structures and processes which the scientist is trying to articulate.[4] Fundamental theoretical insight (often involving mind experiments

9

and imaginative identification with phenomena such as the speed of light), may express this process and underlie such statements as Einstein's, that the discovery of the theory of relativity was due to his having been "so firmly convinced of the harmony of the universe".[5]

Just as each person is a microcosm of the entire universe, he is part of the primordial soul or mystical body of Adam which encompasses all of humanity. Each person (and each nation) has a specific role in the rectification of mankind. Thus it is taught that all languages have their ultimate root in God's Name, and that each is a unique opening to the Infinite.[6] In respect to man, five levels or aspects of consciousness are active, each within the other. The *universal* aspects of consciousness manifest as follows: (a) the innermost spark of divinity (superconsciousness); (b) the "impressions" of previous states of being (including those from the primordial World of Chaos, *Tohu*);[7] and (c) the collective subconscious. The collective subconscious has two aspects: first, that of all humanity (Adam and Eve) which includes an intuitive sense of God; and second, the collective subconscious unique to each people. The two *subjective* aspects of consciousness involve: (d) the unique individual structure of the unconscious as described by the various schools of psychoanalysis; and (e) ordinary awareness.

In relation to the collective subconscious of the Jewish people, it is taught that all of the 600,000 root souls of Israel[8] (including future converts) experienced the direct revelation from God at Mt. Sinai, an experience which became engraved in the psyche.[9] In this regard, the Talmud relates that God went to each of the nations of the world and offered them the Torah; each refused for its own reason. Israel agreed to accept the Torah even before knowing its content. According to Rabbi Elimelech of Lezhensk, there were nevertheless individuals among the nations who agreed to receive the Torah, and there were those among the people of Israel who refused. Those souls who agreed stood with Israel at Mt. Sinai; they are the souls of the future converts to Judaism. Those among the Jewish people who refused are the souls of Jewish proselytes.

It is also taught that another innate characteristic of the Jewish collective subconscious is its willingness to submit to martyrdom (*Kiddush HaShem*; see Ch. III, sect. 1). This aspect of the psyche of the Jewish people is also traced to the experience of the Revelation at Mt. Sinai. According to the Midrash, when the "people saw the sounds" of God's voice [Exod. 20:15], they were unable to endure it and all died. God resurrected all of Israel, who then chose Moses to receive the Torah on their behalf. It is therefore taught that the direct experience of God at Mt. Sinai, as well as the experience of resurrection, is imprinted on the Jewish psyche,[10] and underlies the historical willingness of Jews to die rather than to deny God or their Jewishness.

The profound influence of the unconscious has always been recognized by Judaism, even to the extent that a person was held at least partially responsible for his unconscious acts. In the time of the Temple, for example, a person who committed an unintentional sin was required to bring a sacrifice in atonement. It was recognized that the unconscious or inadvertent act revealed an aspect of his will, and was likely to cause further transgressions unless brought into consciousness. The sin offering is an expression of the basic process of rectification in Judaism. Destructive or chaotic aspects of the unconscious (and according to the *Ari*, of past lives as well) are brought into consciousness where they can be directed into the service of God. This is the foundation in Jewish thought on which Freud built psychoanalysis.[11]

The Jewish view of the microcosmic nature of man underlies the extreme value placed on each individual's life. Each person is called "a small world"; a man who saves another person is likened to one who saves the world. Under Jewish law, therefore, it is forbidden to turn a person over to a mob in order to save even the entire community.[12] The *mitzvah* of saving life (*pikuach nefesh*) overrides all other commandments.[13] The Jewish perspective is that the individual must have the opportunity to achieve his unique potential. Each individual has a definite (and often unknown) *tikkun* or task to achieve in his lifetime. Through the perfection of individuals comes the perfection of the nation, the perfection of humanity, and ultimately, the perfection of existence.

2. The Fall of Consciousness

The fall of Adam expresses the fall of consciousness from its primordial unity into duality ("knowing good and evil"). The dualities of God and man, infinite and finite, essence and form, spiritual and physical, soul and body, life and death, good and evil, are the realities of human consciousness. When unity is categorized into dualities or pluralities, "idols" are potentially created with the power to conceal the fundamental oneness from which they arose. In fact, ordinary awareness cannot grasp the undivided oneness of reality. This is the manifestation in the human mind of the cosmic Breaking of the Vessels. The mind's rational and analytic powers break unity into dichotomies, and then into sub-concepts and elements. What the mind cannot manipulate, define, measure, or duplicate, it tends to reject as unreal. By this largely unconscious strategy the primacy of the ego is maintained.

The battle against "idol worship", against all forms of separation between man and God, has been the Jewish spiritual task since Abraham. The primary idol is the ego from which all other idols such as wealth, beauty, status, and power derive. Powering the ego is the sexual drive, the "all embracing urge". (Rabbi Nachman elaborated that, in the case of highly developed individuals, the drive for power is overriding).[14] The ego, with its "hosts", competes for the person to the extent that where the ego exists, God does not exist. Opposing the primacy of the ego is the fundamental psychological truth of Judaism, that the spark of divinity is the ultimate reality of the psyche.

Glass is a metaphor for purity of consciousness.[15] The refinement of glass from sand (*chol* in Hebrew, which also means "secular" or "ordinary") is a paradigm for the clarification of both consciousness and the physical world. Clarity is receptivity to light, to the life in light. The mind of glass (the mind of the *tzaddik*, the perfected man) has been purified of the distortions of the unconscious and of the "matter" of ego. In terms of the *sefirot*, the quality of glass is *Malchut* of *Malchut*, the ultimate receptive state of consciousness. The essence of truth, therefore, is transparency.

The difference between the state of man before Adam's Fall and after is expressed through the nature of skin. According to the Midrash, the original skin of Adam and Eve was white light (*chashmal*).[16] White represents the highest union, carrying all colors just as silence carries all potentialities of sound.[17] After the primordial sin, God clothed Adam and Eve with "skin clothing". The transformation of light into skin[18] expresses the separation of consciousness from its primordial unity with the divine.[19] Fallen consciousness is light which has become enclothed in increasingly coarse "skins" somewhat analogous to scar tissue. In this respect the only disease mentioned in the Torah is leprosy, the prototypal "skin" disease—the disease of consciousness. The "skin clothing" that replaced Adam's skin of light was the snake's skin.

NOTES

1. "Our likeness" in the verse is often interpreted to refer to the angels. Angels are said to administer the forces of nature. See also n. 2 below.

2. "Three are bound together: God, Torah and Israel" [*Zohar* 3:37a]. One of the ways this effect is discussed is in terms of "angels" which amplify or transmit the effect of actions (including thought) to the higher Worlds. An angel is a force—a spiritual force, a messenger which has no free will of its own. By every *mitzvah* or good deed, and as well, by every bad deed—a man creates an angel. For a useful discussion of this dynamic in modern terms, see Steinsaltz, *The Strife of the Spirit* (Aronson, 1988), Ch. 5.

3. See Ch. V, sect. 2: Reincarnation; and also Ch. VI, sect. 4: Fifth Dimensional, and Messianic Consciousness.

4. According to the *Midrash*, the Torah preceded the Creation of the universe, and is its "blueprint". A Jew is taught the entire Torah *in utero* [*Nidah* 30b]. The Torah he discovers is therefore considered relearning.

The process of scientific inquiry or other types of creative thought in terms of the sefirotic pattern may be described as follows (See Figure 9, Overview):

> The flash of insight or inspiration (*Chochmah*, wisdom or insight) represents the unarticulated insight drawn from the microcosm of the subconscious (*Keter*). This insight or inspiration is then conceptualized and developed in *Binah* (understanding). The *midot* (the seven lower *sefirot*) bring this general hypothesis into specific articulation in respect to all of its implications. Finally, an experiment is formulated, and then performed (*Yesod*; truth in action) to validate the hypothesis formulated in *Binah*. The total theory is expressed in *Tiferet* (Beauty), the holistic center. The results of the experiment are evidenced in *Malchut* (ordinary reality), and are reflected "back up" the *sefirot* for evaluation and reformulation.

5. Quoted in R. Clarke, *Einstein* (World Publishing, 1965), p. 278.

6. The Sages say: "Who is wise? One who learns from all men" [*Sayings of the Fathers 4:1*]. In the Midrash, Elijah says:

> [A]ny human, Jew or Gentile, man or woman, freeman or slave, according to his deeds he can be worthy of the Holy Spirit (*Ruach HaKodesh*)" [*Tana De Bei Eliahu Rabba*].
> 9. See A. Kaplan, *The Bahir* (Weiser, 1979), pp. 156-157.

7. See Overview, sect. 4: The Breaking of the Vessels; and sect. 6: The Rectification of Reality.

8. Kabbalah teaches that in correspondence to the ten *sefirot*, the souls of Israel contain ten archetypal souls (See further Ch. V. n. 15).

In a *minyan* of ten men needed for collective prayer, each of the archetypal souls is represented so as to create a unity:

Keter:	The Heads of Thousands
Chochmah:	The Wise
Binah:	The Understanding
Chesed:	The Bestowers of Kindness
Gevurah:	The Mighty Ones or Warriors
Tiferet:	The Masters of Torah

Netzach:	The Prophets
Hod:	The Seers
Yesod:	The Righteous
Malchut:	The Kings

9. The receiving of the Torah in the collective subconscious underlies the former practice by Jewish courts of forcing a husband by flogging, etc. to "willingly consent" to divorce his wife as required by the law. The unjust husband is considered to be acting against his innate will because he is under the control of his "evil urge". According to Maimonides, the reason that such coercion is justified is in order to compel a husband to do what every Jew subconsciously wishes to do, that is, to live in accordance with the Torah [*Mishnah Torah*, Ch. 2]. See C. Zimmerman, *Torah and Existence* (Jerusalem–New York, 1986), pp. 263-265.

10. In the Talmud it is further stated that: "He who has compassion upon his fellow is known to be descended from Abraham, and he who has no compassion is known not to be descended from the Patriarch" [*Betzah* 32].

11. The healer or psychiatrist possesses the mirror's power to listen and to draw out, and then to reflect the unconscious back to the person—and thus into consciousness. This process is associated with the *sefirah* of *Malchut*, the *sefirah* of self-consciousness—called a reflecting mirror. See Ch. VI, n. 22, and sources cited there in respect to the psychoanalytic movement.

See also, A. Steinsaltz, "Chassidism and Psychoanalysis", in *The Strife of the Spirit* (Aronson, 1988), pp. 187-188.

12. The exception is in the case of a person who has committed a capital offense. For an informed and provocative discussion of the role and status of the individual under *Halachah* in the contemporary context, see Zimmerman, Ibid., especially Ch. III, but also throughout the work.

13. There are three situations in which martyrdom is commanded: idolatry, murder, and adultery. See further, Ch. III, sect. 1: Dying for Truth.

14. See *Basi L'Gani*, Chs. 17-20 (1950) which discusses the drive "to seek victory."

15. The word "glass" in Hebrew is derived from the Hebrew root for "pure". The Talmud analyzes reality using the concepts of purity and impurity, and by definitions of what constitutes a "vessel". Purity/impurity only applies to something which has the status of a vessel. The Rabbis removed glass from the category of "neutral" substances (for example, stone and earth) and placed it in the category of substances which may receive impurity. [*Mishneh Torah, Kelim* 1:5].

16. *Zohar*, Vol. I, 36b, 52b. See Kaplan, *Inner Space* (Moznaim, 1991), pp. 165-176, and pp. 153-155. There, *chashmal* is described as the "vision of nothingness [which] is the color of silence".

Chashmal is interpreted to mean the union of silence and speech, of simultaneous concealment and revelation [*Chagigah* 13b]. In modern Hebrew the word refers to electricity. See Ch. VII, sect. 3: Union.

17. White is obtained when the entire color spectrum is turned rapidly on a

disk. Revolving the colors is elevating them to their origin (*Keter*); mixing is taking them down, eventually to the brown of earth (*Malchut*).

18. In Hebrew, this phenomenon is reflected by the word *or* which means both "skin" and "light". Light is spelled with an *aleph*, skin with an *ayin*. *Aleph* is relatively hidden, soundless; *ayin* phonetically is gutteral. The letter *ayin* represents the coarseness of the *aleph*, its skin or exterior.

19. In the *Havdalah* ceremony that concludes the *Shabbat*, there is a custom to view the translucence of the fingernails against the background of the candlelight as a reminder of the state of Adam's skin before the Fall [*Sefer Bahir* 200].

The Torah given at Mt. Sinai is the healing of the sin of Adam and Eve, the return of man to the Garden. The day of the giving of the Torah is called the "wedding day" on which mankind was again reunited with God [*Ta'anit* 4:8]. Again all were immortal. The souls of the past, present, and future stood together at Sinai enclothed in the light of *chashmal* that enclothed Adam and Eve in the Garden—the light of mystical union.

The sin of the Golden Calf, the equivalent of eating the forbidden fruit, again resulted in the fall of consciousness and loss of immortality for mankind.

Chapter II

Perception

1. Seeing Through the Sefirot

Where the physicist sees the continuous transformation of energy into matter (that is, into various patterns of energy), the kabbalist sees the transformation of light into images purposely created for the eyes of man. Both know that "body", "table", and "mind" are concepts most accurately depicted with inverted commas; that objects are phenomena which exist only in man's perception. The physicist works with four forces of creation (or possibly five), with the expectation that a unified theory (GUT) will be able to articulate these forces as being manifestations of a single force which existed at the very inception of the universe. The kabbalist works with ten forces or creative emanations (the ten *sefirot*), which are also divided into four or five degrees or Worlds of intensity.[1] All of these forces are derived from, and are manifestations of, the one force.

Seeing the world through the *sefirot* means seeing the world as a manifestation of a single unity. Sefirotic perception is holistic and process-oriented. Specific physical phenomena, as well as the individual nature of each person's psyche, are manifestations of various combinations and intensities of the ten forces. (This understanding is embodied in the structure of the Hebrew language, wherein the roots of all words are verbs, that is, processes or combinations of forces. In Hebrew, objects and concepts [nouns] are perceived as permutations of their primary inner processes.) Although the *sefirot* guide and structure perception, each person's seeing is relative to time and place, to the nature of his capabilities and understanding, and to his purpose. Thus the model represented by the ten *sefirot* cannot be used as a stencil; rather, the *sefirot* are best conceived of as a sophisticated symbolic "language" through which reality can be perceived and described.

On the intellectual level, the model and language of the ten *sefirot* (Figures 7-9, Overview) are used to understand the forces at work in ordinary reality, especially in the human psyche. At the most intense levels of consciousness, however, the kabbalist seeks to penetrate beyond the Worlds

16

and the images constructed or projected by the *sefirot*, to the light of Infinity itself.

2. Objective and Subjective Perception

Although the *sefirot* offer a universal language or conceptual framework, human perception remains relative and subjective because it is limited. The idea of objective perception is based on a concept of detachment which the Heisenberg Uncertainty principle in physics has shown to be illusory. Uncertainty exists at the quantum level because the very act of observation is a power that affects what is observed. As will be discussed below, because seeing is both a power and a relationship, distorted vision not only affects the accuracy of perception but also affects (and possibly damages) what is being observed. Thus at the quantum level, as well as at the highest level, that of "God's Face", reality is unknowable.[2]

Ordinarily a person sees what is familiar to his experience, or what is similar to himself. His eyes are at the center of his universe. Ordinary perception could be likened to looking out from within an enclosing cube of mirrors. What one does see is seen through one's own image. Objective vision would be analogous to seeing *through* the mirrors. (Thus seeing through glass is an idiom in the Torah for prophecy.)[3] Destruction of the ego's desires leads to objectivity within the contours of a given psyche, and as well, to the expansion of the potential field of vision. (Even a *tzaddik* who is clear of ego sees through a specific structure of soul.) This is the reason that the inner psychological pre-condition of wisdom or insight (*Chochmah*), is the nullification of ego. A man of insight realizes that his power of sight is not a personal power; and more deeply, sees that he himself and the world are nothing; then deeper, that this nothing is God: "He is the Knowledge, He is the Knower, and He is that which is Known".

The way a person perceives reality is called his kingdom, the *sefirah of Malchut*. Each reality is a way of seeing, an image of knowledge—a kingdom with high physical and psychological walls. Objectivity requires detachment from desire, from one's fear of death, and ultimately, from the fate of one's children.[4] This is one of the major reasons that the sacrifice of Isaac by Abraham is central to Judaism. Jewish spirituality does not seek detachment through renunciation of ordinary life and family but rather through trust in God. That is, Jewish detachment is achieved through the affirmation that no matter what happens, "this also is good." This level of perception, which at its most difficult level involves blessing God even for apparent evil, leads one to the root of reality.[5]

ⵑ Accurate perception is, however, also dependent upon the ability to perceive the extent to which a person or a given thing is fulfilling its purpose. The ability to see purpose depends on the extent that one has actually participated in that purpose. Of itself, detached perception yields a view of meaningless phenomena. A stranger observing a foreign culture sees only the outer manifestations of a hidden dynamic. The foreigner may see the work of political and economic forces or of mere coincidence where the citizen sees the fulfillment of prophecy or of a manifest destiny. A detached observation of a couple pressing their mouths together does not reveal their purpose nor the nature of love. Nor could they prove to such an observer that love objectively exists, nor even describe it. And although they convince him that they feel "love", he might offer alternative psychological or behaviorist interpretations of this experience. The objective observer who rubs his mouth against another person's may prove to himself that love does not exist. Only if he yields his "objectivity" will he eventually love.

Judaism teaches that each person is born to fulfill a specific purpose; that is, to perform a unique role or task connected to the rectification of existence. This role or mission defines his essential being, his true name. The nature of this work or creativity must be discovered by each person for himself, and forms the basis for his own self-perception. If a person's life moves in a direction away from the fulfillment of this purpose, it moves towards meaninglessness and self-betrayal (voluntary exile). The direction of the future is determined by the potential it offers to fulfill his life's work. The past which is meaningful is that which served as a preparation for its achievement. A king (a free man) pursues his own purpose. One who does not serve his own purpose inevitably serves another's (possibly foreign) purpose. He becomes a servant regardless of the level or comfort of his servitude.

In his homeland a person shares the purpose of his people. Political, cultural, and religious divisions reflect aspects of a national soul or character which he cannot deny or cut away from his own. Nevertheless, it is psychologically possible to live in exile in the country of one's birth and to reject one's people. Even in one's own house one may live in exile. Home is the place where there exists a unity of purpose and participation in its achievement; this, in turn, is the most essential definition of marriage. Marriage is both a primordial reunion and a transcendent relationship. A man's true wife or "soul mate" wants for *her own self*, that he achieve his unique purpose. And likewise, a man wants for himself the achievement of his wife's purpose. Marriage means that the man and woman share the same purpose, the same "crown" (*Keter*); that this purpose is the meaning of both their lives, of their one life. Only in this way will they recognize each other as they grow older. Likewise, a person's "children" are not necessarily only the offspring of his or her body. His children are his deeds or creative works, and those who carry on and extend his purpose—those who extend his vision.

3. Male and Female Perception

In Kabbalah, the dynamic and structure of reality are often described using the metaphor of sexuality. The world is made of "lights" and "vessels". The male principle represents light or pure energy, the female represents form and creation. The primordial source of the female principle is the "vacated space" created by the *tzimtzum*, the vessel in which all of existence takes place.[6] The source of the male principle is the ray of the light of Infinity which entered the "womb", and which fills the forms (vessels) of reality (Figure 5, Overview). The terms "male" and "female" are understood archetypally, often in ways that may not conform to the understanding of Western culture. The archetypal male power is that of unlimited giving, associated with water and with the free flow of seed. Love or benevolence (*Chesed*) is considered a male power, while structure and formation (*Gevurah*) is considered female. The archetypal female power is associated with the giving of life, with the formative and nurturing power of the womb. (Eve [*Chavah*] means the mother of all living [Gen. 3:21].) In respect to the mind, the female attracts the "seed" (that is, insight or purpose) to herself, and is "fertilized". Once fertile with the seminal insight from the Father (*Chochmah*), the Higher Mother (*Binah*) gives birth to the complete mental, psychological, and emotional structure which is called "her children".[7]

The male and female principles form indivisible unities or wholes at all levels of existence. Both male and female were created from one origin, the primordial Adam. The phrase in Genesis 22, "He took one of [Adam's] ribs . . ." to form Eve, literally means "one of his sides" (*tzela*)—Adam's left side, the feminine side. The formal sefirotic structure of the psyche of both men and women is the same, although there may be differences in the balance of forces as they manifest in either sex. The psyche of a particular man may express or be dominated by his female powers, and that of a woman by her male powers. (According to the doctrine of reincarnation, it is possible that a male soul live in female body and visa versa).[8] Nevertheless, a holistic understanding would not ignore the mutual influence between the physical body and the psyche. The fact, for example, that a man is unable to bear children and that his body is essentially unchanging (therefore more abstract), is relevant to his whole approach to reality. In their relation to the experience of God, however, all souls become female.[9]

Kabbalah speaks of male and female power as "eyes". A person (man or woman) with a "good female eye" has the power to actualize human potentiality. In regard to a man, for example, the role of the female eye is to rectify and elevate the will of the male towards the achievement of his highest purpose. The woman is therefore called the "crown" of her husband [Prov. 12:4].[10] Abraham represents positive male perception: to see infinity in this world, to see through the world to the divine nothingness (*ayin*). The Sages teach that "he who has a good eye is blessed", and shall bless.[11] Recognizing God in a particular aspect of everyday reality is the very meaning of blessing. Thus the male in oneself guides towards self-nullification. In order to see the *ayin*, one must become as nothing, which is the male gate to the eternal. The female in oneself guides towards the true self, which is the female gate.[12]

Negative male perception is like a ray of entropy: the power to dissolve the bond between elements of meaning, the bond formed through the positive male power of *Chesed* (love).[13] In Judaism, which identifies meaning with speech, this is expressed as the power to break down sentences into words, and to dissect words into isolated letters so that reality appears random and meaningless. Emptiness is "the other side" of the eternal nothingness. Just as projecting the vision of a person's highest self draws him towards that vision, the projection of meaninglessness draws to itself all that is chaotic or negative in the person. The impact of the negative male eye is to destroy competing sources of power or influence, and to cause another to accept the authority of the seer (overseer). The negative aspect of male power is the drive towards domination. As the modern forms of dictatorship demonstrate with their "cults of personality", the primary male idol remains an emperor-god.

The clearest modern example of the "battle of the eyes",[14] as it is sometimes called, was in the concentration camps and ghettos. It was reported that the people best able to retain their humanity (their structure of meaning) against the Nazis' systematic projection of "hell", were those drawing upon a positive ideology or spirituality. Many who did not either came to identify with their Nazi oppressors, or lost their will to live. It seems, however, that once the male "evil eye" has penetrated the inner reality, the elements of meaning in the psyche are not able to stand in the same relationship as before. Even if a person manages to break the "evil eye's" hold, he is vulnerable to despair. His configuration of meaning is held together by will, by the determination to survive and to witness. When this goal in turn becomes meaningless, he may suddenly take his own life.[15]

The negative female power feeds on other lives but is itself barren. (The primordial female fear is to remain empty). The "evil female eye" draws the other into a mirror, a mirror reflecting the other person's self-love, and/or fantasy. Female negative vision draws upon another's need for love and security to create dependency. Female evil, however, remains essentially personal. In contrast, male evil can abstract into a killing force that hunts with bureaucracy, that can administer worlds of the living dead. In both these types of evil, men and women participate.

4. *Seeing with the Eyes of God*

Prophecy means transcending the eyes. Beyond the range of vision is the future, the hidden essence of the present. Seeing the future involves a female power, the power of receiving—the power of faith.[16] For this reason, the Sages consider the level of Sarah's insight and prophecy to be higher than that of Abraham's: "Everything that Sarah says to you listen to her voice" [Gen. 12]. (Similarly, the Midrash interprets "fairest of women" in the Song of Songs [5:9] as referring to the prophets of Israel.)[17] In the *Zohar*, the female is described as eyeless. The prophet sees the flow of providence (the future), as it were, with God's eyes.[18] Seeing the truth depends upon consecration to the infinite, which is related to the covenant of circumcision. The eyes and the lips of the prophet must be circumcised. (The Talmud states that the woman is born circumcised).[19] Eyes which have been circumcised, eyes that are blind and lidless, express the power to see directly into the light.[20]

A process of perception related to that of prophecy is the power of *recognition*. Recognition is the power to perceive the eternal in a person; the seeing through to the root of his soul. In this way, one is seeing him, as far as one is able, as God sees him. One recognizes another by continuously relating to what one perceives to be his highest purpose and aspiration, regardless of the reality at that moment.[21] One uplifts him, loves him—as he is meant to be. Seeing himself through such eyes, those of his friend, teacher, or of his lover, he sees his own worth and beauty. Ultimately, this is a also a person's most profound *self-perception*, the source of his own objectivity towards himself—seeing himself as God sees him.

One's recognition of another is sustained by empathy or compassion, by one's sense of unity with that person. The power to "hover" is the power to embody conflicting states of being; for example, repulsion and love, anger and understanding—seeing the other as he really is, while reflecting the vision of his highest self. Empathy is the ability to identify yet at the same time to remain outside, to touch and to hold back. The power and the size of a person's soul can be spoken of in these terms: the capacity to hold within itself conflicting states of being or consciousness, and yet maintain its own integrity.[22]

"Hovering" implies that one delves only to the level where one is helping the other towards self-recognition. Beyond this, one may reach the level of the other's confusion or inner chaos. Purpose protects the relationship, otherwise one can be drawn into a distorted or even malignant reality. Beyond this point, empathy may turn into a battle of the eyes—into a process of domination on one side, and of entrapment on the other. Chassidism teaches that as soon as one begins to deeply associate with another person, one must be prepared for a lifetime relationship; to "marry" him. The recognition of the other's highest self that is founded on the long-term commitment to care makes the highest relationship achievable: man and nature, parent and child, master and disciple, friendship, love between a man and a woman.

In relation to the land of Israel, recognition means recognizing the land's unique function and relation to the Jewish people, and also to other peoples and their visions of the land. In its highest sense, "possession"—whether it be the land of Israel or any other loved one—means a relationship of ever deepening recognition. Through the eyes of the visionary pioneers the land blossomed like a woman in love. The Jewish people have always possessed Zion because they have held the image of its transcendent purpose, of their unity of purpose.

NOTES

1. See Overview, sect. 2: The Five Worlds; and sect. 3: The Ten *Sefirot*.

2. Many see in the illusory and transitory nature of quantum phenomena proof of the ultimate arbitrariness of human existence. The kabbalist might see this unpredictability as the physical root of the freedom of choice. Uncertainty as to God's presence in the world is the prerequisite for free will (see Overview, sect. 5: Evil and Free Choice). In this view, God's hiddenness or self-restraint is built into the quantum level of reality, implying that uncertainty is a purposeful dimension built into the very structure of the physical world.

See Steinsaltz, *The Strife of the Spirit*; Ibid., pp. 31-32, for a discussion of the Uncertainty Principle and divine providence.

Kabbalah would agree with Wigner's statement that "it is not possible to formulate the laws of [quantum theory] without reference to consciousness". E.P. Wigner, *Symmetries and Reflections*, Scientific Essays (MIT Press, 1970), p. 172.

Books such as F. Capra's, *The Tao of Physics* (Bantam, 1984, 2nd ed.), and the writings of David Bohm are useful to gain an appreciation of the parallels between Kabbalah and modern scientific thought. Most of the popular books linking mysticism and physics do not refer to Kabbalah but rather to the better known of the Eastern mystical traditions. Nevertheless, much of what is said in this context is relevant.

3. Only Moses saw through transparent glass [*Yevamot 49b*]; that is, nothing in his prophecies was left to his subjective interpretation. All of the other prophets saw through unclear or translucent glass. For this reason, Jewish law—other than in the case of Moses—is not based on the prophets.

See further in respect to the "cube" analogy, Ch. VI: The Mind of the Tzaddik.

4. The following is reported by Rabbi Zvi Hirsch Meisels in his volume of responsa from Auschwitz. He reports that on the eve of Rosh Hashanah in 1944, the Nazi commander determined to kill all the boys not big enough to work. A post with a vertical bar was set up at a predetermined height; each boy was forced to pass under the bar. Those who tried to stretch on their tiptoes were bludgeoned to death on the spot. At the end of the *selektion*, the 1400 boys who had not passed were imprisoned in a separate cellblock under the guard of kapos. They were to receive no further food or drink until their execution. The next morning, the first day of Rosh Hashanah, fathers and other relatives who still had something of value tried frantically to bribe the kapos to release their sons. The kapos agreed to be bribed on condition that other boys be first caught in order to replace those who would be freed. The Nazis had counted and would hold them responsible for the exact number.

Rabbi Meisels was approached by a Jew from Oberland with a question of Jewish law (*Halachah*). Could he save his son's life at the expense of another boy's life? Rabbi Meisels refused to give an answer and begged not to be asked this question but the father took it that it was forbidden by *Halachah*. In fact, if it were certain that another boy would be killed in his son's place, it was indeed forbidden.

Rabbi Meisels reports that throughout the day of Rosh Hashanah, the man was joyful and declared that he accepted that his only son will lose his life according to the Torah and *Halachah*. And that the father prayed openly . . . "that his act might be acceptable in the sight of the Almighty as Abraham's binding of Isaac". Reported in I. Rosenbaum, *Holocaust and Halachah* (Ktav, 1976), pp. 3-5.

5. The Talmud teaches that "in this world we must bless God both for good and evil. But in the World to Come, we will realize that there is nothing but good" [*Pesachim* 50a].

6. See Overview, sect. 1: Creation, and the *Tzimtzum*. The word for female, *nekiva*, is derived from the root meaning an opening, a hole—a potential vessel.

7. The left side of the *sefirot* is considered female, the right side male; the center is the channel of their union or reconciliation in terms of purpose, leading to action. These form the basic synergistic dynamic of the *sefirot*.

Friendship is the middle line, running back and forth between male and female aspects. See Overview, sect. 3: The Tree of Life, the Ten *Sefirot*.

8. See generally in this regard, Ch. V, sect. 2: Reincarnation, in particular, n. 19.

9. The root of the feminine is "simple faith" (the highest dimension of *Keter*, *Radlah*), which expresses the receptive power beyond mind.

Keter (Crown) is the highest level of the *sefirot* and is identified with the supreme will and purpose. *Keter* is the *sefirah* through which the light of Infinity (Or *Ain Sof*) emanates into the other *sefirot*. It is "closest" to the source and is the most hidden.

The *Zohar* states that even though *Keter* is the most brilliant light, it is utter darkness compared to the Infinite Being. *Keter* is above mind, and can be referred to as the deepest levels of the subconscious, or as superconsciousness. It is also called *ayin* (divine nothingness), the root or inner essence of all the other *sefirot*.

10. "Who is a good woman? She who does her husband's will". The Sages explain that the verb "to do" (*la'asot*) means "to rectify". Thus Chassidism teaches that a good woman rectifies her husband's will [*Likutei Sichot*, Vol. 4, p. 1069]. "If he merits, she aids him; if not, she opposes him" [*Yevamot* 63a].

11. *Sotah* 38b interpreting Prov. 22:9.

12. As a contrast in spiritual approach, for example, Braslav Chassidism may be considered more female; to be more internal and self-reflective. In contrast, Chabad Chassidism tends to be more male; to concentrate on getting out of the self, on "knowing before whom one stands". Nevertheless, each approach is dependent upon the other, and is contained within the other.

13. In the primordial world of *Tohu* (Chaos), each element of Creation was separate and none would combine. God destroyed that world and created the new order with love (*Chesed*), the male quality that draws disparate elements into union. (On the level of the physical universe, this is expressed by attractive forces such as gravity). See Overview, sect. 4: The Breaking of the Vessels, and sect. 6: The Rectification of Reality.

14. In the context of normal living, the business world is considered the primary arena of the "duel of eyes". The original bad eye and good eye are Abraham and Ephron, from whom Abraham bought the burial cave of Machpelah in Hebron for Sarah. Ephron is the first man in Torah with whom there is a commercial transaction. (Ephron's name is equal in *gematria* to "bad eye"; see n. 16 below on *gematria*).

Business is a model for all relationships; how one conducts business is a test as to how one sees "the real world". According to Kabbalah, the source of earning a living is the Unknowable Head of *Keter* (*Radlah*), which is simple faith, and the primordial root of the female soul (See n. 9 above). The level of *Radlah* in *Keter* is the level of, and the power to achieve the unity of opposites.

To do business properly means "to give and to take in faith" (*nose v'notain b'emunah*). "Taking" (buying) means to lift up; the term *nose* (giving, selling) is used to indicate the power to unite opposites (it is from the same root as the word for "marriage"). The Sages teach that whoever gives should "give with a goodly eye"; that is, that one's selling should be a blessing to the buyer. Buying is the lifting up of the purchase to the state of unity.

This is one of the reasons a man's business success or failure is linked to the soul of his wife or soul mate [*Berachot* 17a]. Improper business dealings are compared to going to a house of prostitution to make money or to "marrying a prostitute" [*Vayikra Rabba* 15:6]. Money, which like glass is connected to the *sefirah* of *Malchut*, is both transparent and reflective—it is an image which has no value or meaning of its own. In the eyes of one who is not clear of ego, money is his mirror; in the eyes of a kabbalist, money indicates the flow of energy.

The *Halachah* pertaining to business opposes the view that business is a type of war. *Caveat emptor* is not a Jewish concept. Very stringent limitations are set on the amount of profits that can be earned (e.g., 1/6th for essential commodities), false or misleading advertising, ruinous competition, charging of interest, employee protection, exploitation of the environment, etc. The controls stated in the *Halachah* are generally more strict than the prohibitions found in much of the modern consumer protection and regulatory legislation. On Jewish law and modern business see: A. Levine, *Economics and Jewish Law* (Ktav, 1987); and more generally, A. Levine, *Free Enterprise and Jewish Law* (Ktav, 1980); and M. Tamari, *With All Your Possessions* (The Free Press, 1987).

15. Three tragic examples are the Jewish writers Paul Celan, Primo Levi, and most recently, Jerzy Kosinski.

16. The word "kabbalah" is from the Hebrew root meaning to receive, and is used in the *Gemara* to refer to the prophetic books of the Bible. On the other hand, many kabbalists have used "prophecy" as a general term to describe various types of mystical experience. The two words "wisdom" (*Chochmah*) and "prophecy" (*Nevua; Binah*) together equal in *gematria* "Kabbalah", and also equal the word "grace" (*chein*). Thus Kabbalah is called the knowledge (*Da'at*) of grace.

Gematria is a method of Torah interpretation used extensively in Kabbalah. According to the *Zohar*, it represents one of the seven levels of the Torah interpretation. *Gematria* is the numerical analysis of words and letters; each letter of the alphabet has a numerical equivalent. The basic premise is that, as the world was spoken into existence by God, the underlying unity of existence is embodied in the Hebrew language itself. Therefore, if one word or phrase in the Torah equals or is related to another numerically, then they are connected in meaning.

The kabbalist uses *gematria* as a tool to deepen awareness of relationships and to reveal nuances. The proper application of *gematria* is to reveal the structural beauty of Torah. If a new association presents itself, a kabbalist might test and "play" with it using *gematria*. If the new idea yields beautiful *gematriot*, this fact would be taken to support and then to deepen the new insight by expanding the lattice of relationships. Certain *gematriot* are compelling, others are disregarded.

17. *Shemot Rabbah* 1:1.

18. All prophecy is associated with the *sefirot* of *Netzach* and *Hod*. These *sefirot* correspond to the two cherubim which stood over the Arc of the Tabernacle, and later in the Temple.

According to the Sages, prophecy in the strict Biblical sense, lasted one thousand years in Israel from the time of the Exodus until forty years after the building of the Second Temple (313 B.C.E.). Prophecy ceased after the last of the prophets, Haggai, Zechariah, and Malachi all died in a single month. The Sages say that prophecy depends on the connection to the Land of Israel. The *Sefer Kuzari* of Rabbi Yehuda Ha Levi holds that prophecy will only be restored when the majority of Jews are living there.

19. *Avodah Zarah* 27a. Lips are the mouth's eyelids; eyelids are the eyes' lips. In terms of the *sefirot*, both the eyelids and the lips are associated with *Netzach* and *Hod*.

20. Ps. 121:4; *Likutei Torah* 5:14b.

21. Not every perception is the same; the *tzaddik* projects the other's eternal nature, but the person who hates is also clear. An enemy projects the negative image. It is said in Chassidism that he who hates you most, also sees you.

22. Compassion is the inner attribute of the *sefirah* of *Tiferet* (beauty), the center or "heart" of the *sefirot*. *Tiferet* is the *sefirah* that is in connection with all of the others yet expresses the identity of the whole as an entirety. See Overview, Figure 7.

CHAPTER III

Truth

1. Dying for Truth

Man's commitment to truth is an expression of his innate loyalty to a higher purpose and authority. In the imagery of Kabbalah, this is expressed as the firmness of the father's *brit* [meaning both the procreative organ and the covenant] extending into the *brit* of the son: the father's will extending into the son's, the father's eternality extending into the son's, the Infinite purpose extending through the son. Thus when a person is realizing the truth, he is hearing his most intimate name being called.[1]

Kiddush HaShem (martyrdom) is the supreme moment of truth. In the Jewish view, individual survival is not the highest value. Ultimately, truth is more important. The *sefirah* of *Netzach*, which means both "victory" and "eternity", expresses the victory of the consciousness of eternity over death. Victory—because the truth is that man is light. The inner attribute of *Netzach*, therefore, is "security"; security in the face of death, which can only be found in the eternal. Just as the call of truth is the father calling his son's name, at the moment of martyrdom, the son or daughter calls back.[2]

Kiddush HaShem is the ultimate *mitzvah*, the most *potent* act because of its power to regenerate itself—to give birth in others to the awareness of its truth. As the witness records the dance, and as the survivors find the pages that were hidden in the ground, and as the printers publish it, and as the author retells it to you, the seed of truth passes through the generations:[3]

> . . . Reb Shlomo Zhelichovsky, his father-in-law Benyamin Rudol, Berl Wolfish, Mordechai Morgenstern, Shlomo Gershonovitch and five other Jews whose names are unknown—were arrested for no reason, and at noon on the eve of *Shavuot* the entire Jewish population must assemble in the market where there is a gallows . . . The ghetto is opened for non-Jewish children to also attend. Reb Shlomo Zhelichovsky calls out to all the gathered to help him and his fellow martyrs by not displaying sorrow . . . he takes his fellow Jews in a

[dance] circle and tells them, "The only thing the *Yetzer Ha'ra* [evil] can want
of us—is for us to be sad and angry with the Creator. . . . [After being beaten
by the SS] he continues to sing Kaddish to the melody of the Yom Kippur
Neilah prayer—and cries out "*Shema Yisrael*" (Hear, O Israel) and *HaShem hu
Elokim* (the Lord is God) seven times . . . and gives up his soul on the altar of
Kiddush HaShem. . . . (Zdunska-Wola, in the year 5702 [1942])

Kiddush HaShem is the testimony that the evil that is happening is not
as real as the goodness of God. The SS men who are now all-powerful will
disappear. To become angry with God is to prove that evil is more real
than God; to be afraid is to prove that one's ego is more real than God.
Kiddush HaShem is considered an innate characteristic of the Jewish soul
because truth is its very purpose. This power to withstand the ultimate test,
to give one's life rather than renounce one's Jewishness, is not confined to
the great ones.[4] The millions of martyrs, their loyalty to the truth of Israel
through a hundred generations, is the *brit* of the fathers. The diamond core
of the Jewish people.

2. The Man of Actions

The truth of the Torah is expressed in people. The Sages themselves
are called the living Torah. The perfected man is the whole man, the man
able to act (to effect rectification) in many dimensions and aspects of life.
(The Hebrew word for "perfect" is derived from the root meaning "whole",
shlemut.) An idea which is not realized in action is not true: it is only potentially true. (One whose Torah is mere scholarship is not considered
a "scholar".) The daily actions of the Sages have the status of Torah; their
personal actions can be a source of binding laws. The Talmud relates how
students used to study the scholar's every action, even to the extent of how
he acted in conjugal relation to his wife. Similar stories are told in respect
to the chassidic Rebbes. As the Sages said of themselves:[5]

The deliberate errors of the unlearned are regarded as unintentional, while the
unintentional mistakes of the scholars are regarded as deliberate.

True action is clear not only in intention but also in form. Thus even proper
actions which are nevertheless capable of being misinterpreted by ordinary
people, and thereby to cast shame on the Torah, are considered a blas-
phemy (*hillul HaShem*).[6]

The *potency* of an act refers to its power to reproduce itself through
the generations and thus to perpetuate its purpose. (This is the spiritual

analogue to the perpetuation of gene characteristics.) The potency of an act depends upon its objectivity, upon the degree to which it is clear of desires—even of the desire for spiritual advancement. Only one desire creates complete clarity: to act for the sake of the Name (*l'shmah*).[7] One acts because that is what should be done. It is then up to the flow of the universe. A person's action arouses or frees the universe to act. Such an act will be more powerful than the effort expended because it advances the divine purpose. The direction of true action, therefore, is always towards the creation of a higher synthesis or unity.

An act which is *l'shmah* becomes impersonal, or more precisely, transpersonal. Such acts express man's collaboration in the perfection of the Creation. Each act performed *l'shmah* becomes a ritual of consecration, and in a sense, a personal sacrifice. Before performing a *mitzvah*, the kabbalist declares his intention that his action be: ". . . For the sake of the union of the Holy One, blessed be He, with His *Shechinah*, in the name of all Israel".[8] That his action bring about the union of the hidden and the revealed worlds, the union of the eternal and ordinary life.

Not only is a man not living truth to the extent that he desires but also to the extent that he fears. The fear of death is the primary expression of the ego. Adam fell, and he knew death; that is, he feared death. Fear is an essential characteristic of ordinary consciousness; not only fear of death but also fear of physical suffering, of rejection, of failure, etc. If one continually conquers his ego, he conquers his fear. One who conquers the fear of death fears only God, that he will be cut off from God. Or more exactly, that he will cut himself off.[9] This is the spiritual analogue to the fear of physical death.[10]

Saintliness (*tzaddikut*) is associated with the *sefirah* of *Yesod* (truth in action), which corresponds to the procreative organ in the body.[11] The term *"tzaddik"* is reserved for one who has conquered his sexual urge, which Kabbalah recognizes to be the primary root of all psychic drives and desires. Just as the fear of death is the primary source of fear, the sexual drive is the primary source of desire. Joseph is called *"tzaddik"* by the Rabbis because when he saw the vision of his father Jacob before him, he withstood the extreme sexual temptation of Potiphar's wife.[12]

A clear expression of what is meant by true action is seen concretely in the *mitzvah* of charity. *Tzedakah* (charity) is from the same Hebrew root meaning "justice" (*tzeddik*), and also *"tzaddik"*. The *mitzvah* of charity is based on emulation of God's way: "You open your hand and satisfy the desires of all living creatures" [Ps. 145:16]. Even those receiving charity are therefore required to give charity. (According to *Halachah*, a person should give at least 10 percent and preferably 20 percent of his net income to charity.) In the writings of Maimonides, the following reflects the progression of the element of *l'shmah*, and therefore the order of preference in respect to charitable acts:

> The highest form of charity is to provide the means for a person to make an independent living—to give of oneself. These means include loans, investment in a new business, grants, employment, and entering into partnership;
>
> Charity given in complete anonymity where neither side knows the identity of the other;
>
> Charity given where the donor knows the recipient but the recipient does not know the donor;
>
> Charity where the recipient knows the donor but the donor does not know the recipient;
>
> Giving to the needy before he requests it;
>
> Giving after a request;
>
> Giving less than one should but in a cheerful manner;
>
> Giving ungraciously.[13]

3. True Actions: Mitzvot (Commandments)

The purpose of the *mitzvot* (commandments) is to raise the individual, and by so doing, to raise all of existence into total consciousness. Thus Rav Abraham Isaac Kook states,[14]

> Whenever a person raises himself through good deeds, through a higher . . . yearning for Godliness, for wisdom, justice, beauty and equity, he perfects thereby the spiritual disposition of all existence. All people become better in their inwardness through the ascendency of the good in any one of them . . . and thus all existence becomes ennobled and more exalted.

The dynamic underlying the above statement is based on the microcosmic nature of existence. As mentioned above (Ch. I, sect. 1), Kabbalah teaches that each of the 620 letters of the Ten Commandments is the ultimate root of each of the *mitzvot* (the 613 commandments of the Torah together with the seven Rabbinic injunctions).[15] In turn, each of the 613 *mitzvot* is related to a specific aspect of the human body, of the soul, and of the universe itself. This correspondence reflects the microcosmic or holographic nature of reality in which the body, the psyche, the soul, and the universe are isomorphically related or are images of each other. The *mitzvot* define the objective channels of relationship between these levels of existence.

The *mitzvot* apply to three general areas of relationship: man and God (e.g., *teffilin*, prayer), man and humanity (e.g., to love one's neighbor as oneself), man and Creation. In respect to the *mitzvot* relating to the Creation, for example, a person must care for his own physical safety and keep his body healthy. (Accordingly, some hold that smoking is against *Halachah*.) Under the same logic, the physical environment must also be protected against exploitation and pollution. It has been argued that it is a Halachic requirement that the most efficient methods of production be employed in all areas of endeavor in order to preserve the world.[16] This three-way partnership between man, the Creation, and God is constantly reinforced and intensified by the many blessings which arise as a person lives day by day, hour by hour. These blessings (set by the Sages to be one hundred a day),[17] formalize opportunities to regain consciousness at the key points and meetings in the routine of ordinary living.

Halachah is the revelation of Mt. Sinai *expressed in actions*. The total structure or way of the *mitzvot* is revealed from the inside out; from its hidden source in infinity, it flows "out" into the revealed world. Thus it is taught that the Ten Commandments were first pronounced as one word.[18] Only a person who is participating in the purpose of Torah, who is "hearing" the revelation of Mt. Sinai in his daily life, perceives its inner dynamic. This is the basis for the Jewish approach of prior commitment: *act* and then one hears.[19]

The *mitzvot* have been likened to a system of channels through which the current of the divine will flows into daily life. A person does not create the current, he merely allows it to flow. It is God's power flowing through the *mitzvot* that perfects the individual and existence. As discussed above, to the extent that the act is performed "for the sake of the Name (*l'shmah*)", the more powerful its impact. The *mitzvot* are therefore the forms through which a life of self-negation (*bitul*) is lived. (Nevertheless, precisely through this process of self-negation, a person's unique character will come to expression.) Ideally, each *mitzvah* involves two stages: the first is a reflection or meditation on the divine, the second is the act itself. The purity of the intention and the exactness with which a *mitzvah* is performed determine the intensity and, therefore, the effectiveness of the rectification. The perfection of the act of the *mitzvah* is its truth. Thus much of the actual service or practice of the kabbalist is concerned with the proper mystical intention (*kavannah*) with which each particular *mitzvah* is to be performed.

The *mitzvot* are divided into positive and negative commandments. The purpose of the negative *mitzvot* (*lo tase*; not to be done) is to separate a person from that which will separate him from the awareness of God. The purpose of the positive injunctions is to bring him closer.[20] The positive *mitzvot* are modes of contact with the divine; the negative prohibitions repudiate idolatry in all its possible forms. These are the first two commandments: "I am the Lord your God . . .", and "Thou shall have no other gods besides me . . ." [Exodus 20: 2-3]. To the extent that a man follows the path of the *mitzvot*, he can expect to be brought closer to God through all of his actions.

4. Truth and Love

In the moment of absolute truth, one experiences a free-falling through the past and future. This is the experience of the center line in the *sefirot*, the channel through which the infinite (*Keter*) manifests in finite reality (*Malchut*). Truth is the experience of future fusing with past, the moment of unity.[21] Truth is unceasing and timeless; what is temporary or is capable of being interrupted is, to that extent, not true. This is the Jewish understanding of what is "alive" or "living"; only what is true is called "alive".

According to the *Midrash*, when God wanted to create Adam, two powers came before Him: *Chesed* (love, or kindness) and *Emet* (truth).[22] Love was for the creation of Adam because the world was made of love. Truth was against because the world of ordinary consciousness is its antithesis, the "world of lies".[23] In the world there is no absolute truth, only probabilities and relativities. Absolute truth is captured in time and space, in the part-truth of words, in images (objects), in the finite structure of the mind. The nature of truth is to dissolve the world;[24] when a statement or action reveals the truth, it reveals the infinite light-essence of its subject. At the very least, every person, object, or subject is seen as an aspect of a more fundamental reality. In truth, nothing has independent existence. "Truth is one and only one".[25]

In the idiom of the *Midrash*, in order to create the world, the Creator had to thrust truth down, to make truth submit to love. God created the world with the power of love, and because of His love [Psalms 89:3]. More fundamental than the truth that all is light, is the truth of the love of God. To the extent that truth would dissolve ordinary reality by affirming only the reality of the Source, truth denies God's love and purpose for the Creation. The light of Infinity itself is but an image of God's love.

NOTES

1. According to Rashi, Joseph was able to resist the sexual temptation of Potiphar's wife when, at the very last moment, an image of his father, Jacob, appeared to him.

The experience that one has when one realizes the truth is an experience related to that of the animals named by Adam. Adam called each animal species by its true name, and its unique essence was revealed. (This is the analogue to the process of "recognition" discussed above; see Ch. II, sect. 4).

2. At the moment of martyrdom, a Jew calls out: "Hear, O Israel, the Lord is Our God, the Lord is One."

3. Recorded in *Selected Documents from the Warsaw Ghetto Underground Archives*, edited by J. Kermish (Yad Vashem: Jerusalem, 1986, p. 423).

4. Even when a Jew is killed "unconsciously"—that is, unwillingly but because he is a Jew—he is considered to have performed the *mitzvah*. It is held, however, that if he professes disbelief at the time of death, it is not considered a *mitzvah*.

5. *Bava Mitziah* 33b; *Sanhedrin* 103b.

6. *Yoma* 76a. See A. Steinsaltz. *The Essential Talmud* (Basic Books, 1976), Ch. 33: "What Is a Scholar".

7. On the other hand, the Talmud says that doing a *mitzvah* is valuable in itself. *Mitzvot* not performed for the sake of the Name will eventually become *l'shmah*. This position also recognizes the philosophical and psychological difficulties in determining a completely selfless act.

8. This is an abbreviated form of a longer declaration found in the writings of the Ari. For comment, see for example, *Tanya*, Ch. 41.

9. Fear of being cut off from God by committing a sin or otherwise, is a spiritually positive aspect of fear (*Yirat Shamaim*). See further, Ch. VI, sect. 1.

10. Metamorphosis from the state of fear to the state of freedom is through laughter. When a person who is afraid of dying suddenly sees the truth, fear becomes laughter. In Kabbalah, the three patriarchs, Abraham, Isaac, and Jacob, are related to the three dimensions of reality: space, time, and soul. About Isaac, who is related to the dimension of time, there is the expression, *pachad Yitzchak*, the fear of Isaac. Yitzach means "shall laugh", expressing the secret of the transition from this world of fear to the laughter of the World to Come. The relief of laughter expresses a moment of truth, a moment of liberation. Isaac, who at the time of the sacrifice of Isaac by Abraham was thirty-seven years old, yielded to his father's authority (purpose) on Mt. Moriah. By giving up his hold on time Isaac achieved laughter, the mastery over time.

The verse, "She laughs at the last day", from *Eshet Heil* ("A Woman of Valor"; Prov. 31) is interpreted to mean, "she laughs at death".

11. *Zohar* 3:11b. *Yesod* literally means foundation. "The *tzaddik* is the foundation of the world" [Prov. 10:25].

Yesod is the sense of where in reality to achieve one's purpose, where to set the foundation. *Yesod* is wedged into *Malchut* (reality, the earth, the woman). Where to build is considered a masculine sense.

12. *Sotah* 36b.

13. The essence of charity is the life force that a person has invested in order to earn the money—his own self-sacrifice. *Tanya*, Ch. 37; *Shulchan Aruch*, Ch. 249, parag. 6-13; Maimonides, *Yad Hazakah* 10: 7-12. See M. Tamari, *With All Your Possessions: Jewish Ethics and Economic Life* (The Free Press, 1987), Chs. 3 and 9.

14. Rav Kook, *Orot HaKodesh*, quoted in Bokser, *Abraham Isaac Kook* (Paulist Press, 1978), p. 24.

15. *Tanya*, Ch. 53. Learning Torah is the most all-inclusive of the *mitzvot* because it motivates performance of all of the others: "Great is learning for it leads to doing" [*Kiddushin* 40b].

The seven Rabbinic *mitzvot* are: *Shabbat* candles, *Chanukah* candles, Blessings, washing hands, reading of the *Megillah*, saying the *Hallel, and Eruv* (*Shabbat* borders).

16. See Levine, *Economics and Jewish Law* (Ktav, 1987); and *Free Enterprise and Jewish Law* (Ktav, 1980).

17. *Menachot* 43b.

18. *Mechilta* to Exod. 20:1.

19. See further, Ch. VIII, sect. 2: Seeding (*na'ase v'nishma*). See also, Steinsaltz, *The Long Shorter Way*; Ibid., pp. 288-289.

20. The positive commandments may be further classified according to the *sefirot*. Those *mitzvot* associated with the right side are rooted in giving (Kindness, *Chesed*); those on the left involve restraint or "severity" (*Gevurah*)—including acts of ritual, judgment, and worship. The *mitzvot* of the center line (*Tiferet*, beauty, harmony, compassion), for example, are concerned with Torah study, physical love, etc.

21. *Da'at*, which is the interface between the past (*Chochmah*) and future (*Binah*), expresses the temporal "now" by externalizing the timelessness of the *ayin* (*Keter*).

As well, this is seen in the word for truth *emet* (alef-mem-tav), which includes the first, middle and last letters of the Hebrew alphabet. As such, they refer to the past, present, and future. See Kaplan, *The Bahir*, Ibid., pp. 107, 119. See further, Ch. IV, sect. 1: Time.

22. *Bereishit Rabba* 8:5.

23. *Tanya*, Ch. 6. "Any lie that does not have a little truth in it at the beginning will not endure in the end." Rashi to Num. 13:27.

24. From the human perspective, there are two levels of truth. The lower level is that in every person or object there is a "spark" of divine origin which is its life force. The spark that is liberated by recognition of this truth leaves the shell behind, as the soul leaves the body behind in the grave. The higher level of truth is that all reality is divine, the "shell" as well as the "captured" spark.

25. Only simple faith can embrace the whole truth. Faith, the infinite receptivity beyond mind, is the ultimate potential of human consciousness.

CHAPTER IV

Returning Home

1. Time

Birth and Death

According to Chassidic understanding, a completely new world is continuously reborn from nothingness—pulsing instantaneously, into and out of existence. There is no continuity between one moment and the next other than God's purpose. Each moment is the image of all that God wills to exist. The influence of the divine purpose may be likened to a pervasive draw towards perfection, a draw which may be temporarily overcome by the power of free choice. (The independence of the power of free will is itself a manifestation of God's will.) A person feels this draw within himself as his innate love of perfection, and as his drive towards immortality.

Judaism does not relate to time as a death process. (The law of entropy applies only to a closed system.) The universe is a system open to an infinite source of renewal; new potentiality (new choice) is created each moment. Time is therefore the process of perfection; the body is not its measure.[1] Each soul continues until the "end of days", until the perfection of all existence. For the individual, the true measure of time is the degree to which his or her life purpose has been achieved. Likewise, on the plane of history, time is measured by the degree existence has been rectified. Time moves faster and slower; the process of *tikkun* advances and retreats, "every seeming descent is part of a greater ascent". Rav Kook describes this dynamic of history:[2]

> Nothing remains the same; everything blooms, everything ascends, everything steadily increases in light and truth. The enlightened spirit does not become discouraged even when he discerns that the line of ascendence is circuitous, including both advances and declines, a forward movement but also fierce retreats, for even the retreats abound in the potential for future progress.

35

In the mind of ordinary reality, the parameters of the experience of time are birth and death. A "time to die" is born simultaneously with a "time to live". The idea of time as being the interval between one's birth and death is called the fruit of the Tree of Knowledge of Good and Evil. When Adam ate the fruit of the Tree of Knowledge, he separated himself from the primordial unity and identified with his brain and body. As the mental structure in the brain is finite, and as the material of the body is dissolvable, his awareness fell into finitude. Self-consciousness became his exile, his mortality. Exile can extend to a man's thinking of himself as an absurd, isolated thought in a meaningless Cosmos. Although such a person may live a life of high ethical concern and of compassion for others, from his existential perspective, time is death.

Rabbi Nachman teaches that each person must seek "long life" by "extending his days". By this is meant to "extend his days" with awareness of infinity, to extend time (to be free of time) by expanding the mind's borders. "Long life" may begin with awareness of the infinity of the physical universe. As Einstein said of himself, "The contemplation of the Cosmos beckons like a liberation"; it beckons because the infinite is home. When a Jew dies, he re-enters the womb of eternal Israel. ("Lying down in the grave" is an idiom of the Sages for the seed re-entering the womb.)[3] A person dies into the arms of his Mother, who herself lies in the arms of God: this is his home within his home.

Shalom

In Ecclesiastes, time begins with birth and ends with peace. (There are twenty-eight different "times" described in fourteen pairs of opposites.) The last pair is ". . . a time of war, and a time of peace (*shalom*)" [Eccles. 3:1]. This final war consists of two battles: the first for the rectification of the mind, the last for the rectification of physical reality. The two "battles" together constitute the war of Messiah, the war to reunify existence. According to the *Midrash*, the world was created with the letter *beth* (the first letter of *bereshit*, genesis), which has three lines representing the three dimensions of space. The first victory of the Messiah will be the "building" of its fourth side, forming the square of the final *mem*, the last letter of *shalom* (peace). ("Peace" is from the Hebrew root meaning "perfect" and "whole"). *Shalom* is life in the eternal present, the rectification of the fourth dimension of time. Thus the preliminary process of the Messiah can be thought of as dissolving the mind's idea of death. The idea of time lasts only as long as the idea of death. *Shalom* (the perfected state of the *sefirah* of *Malchut*) is what is meant by the Garden of Eden.

The entire *Mishnah* concludes by saying that God did not find a vessel worthy to hold blessing except *shalom*. The blessing which only *shalom* is worthy to receive is the life of the Messiah, the most radical and revolutionary life imaginable. The purpose of Adam's life in the Garden before the Fall was to reach messianic consciousness. The war of the Messiah is the struggle of a new dimension to be born, the fifth and highest level of soul (*yechida*) (See further, Ch. VI, sect. 3). Just as the fourth dimension of time "liberates" three dimensions of physical space, that is, reveals previously unimaginable relationships and potentialities, the fifth dimension liberates pure beingness.

2. Returning Home: The Circles and Rhythms of Tshuvah

The End Enwedged into the Beginning

The experience of returning moves in two directions towards the one home: return to the primordial root of existence, and return to the World to Come. The Garden of Eden is the consciousness that comes into being when these two returns are one. To Rabbi Amorai's question, "Where is the Garden of Eden?" the Sefer Bahir replies, "It is on earth";[4] that is, within day-to-day reality. The circle of consciousness is represented by the Hebrew letter *samech* [O], which expresses the basic kabbalistic concept of the "end enwedged into the beginning, and the beginning into the end". This is the meaning of Rabbi Nachman's saying, "A Jew remembers the future, the World to Come".

In Ecclesiastes [1:1-7], the philosophy of the meaningless circle is defined:

[A]ll is vanity . . . generations go and generations come. . . . The sun rises and the sun sets and aspires to its place to rise again. . . . The wind whirls round and round, returning again in accordance within its circles. . . .

The end of Ecclesiastes reads:

[T]he end (*sof*) of the matter . . . fear God and keep his commandments, for this is all of man.

The word *sof*, which begins with the circle of the *samech*, symbolizes the end "of the matter"; the end of empty existence enwedging into the beginning of the return.

There are two mutually dependent paths of return. The lower return home is the "return from fear" (*tshuvah m'yira*) alluded to above in Ecclesiastes. To "fear God" has many meanings and levels; in this context, fear means to become aware (See further, Ch. VI, sect. 1). The lower return begins when a person realizes that his life is somehow futile or meaningless; that is, that he is living the life of an exile.[5] No matter how outwardly successful, a person may realize that he is betraying himself. ("Egypt" refers to all captivities, to all states of exile—physical, psychological, and spiritual.) In exile, authentic self-expression is of one's self-contradiction and absurdity, of one's mistaken identity. The turn of the *ba'al tshuvah* (literally, the master of return or of response)[6] is the expression of a powerful and (what may appear to be) ruthless ambition to be true to himself.

The lower return is from the "lying" which characterizes psychic and spiritual disharmony. Returning to oneself is returning to the eternal in oneself. The process of return unifies a person's character (his mind and emotions) with his actions, thus progressively establishing the integrity of the self.[7] (A person who is himself is doing his or her real work, in the right place, and is married to his destined partner.) One becomes true by recognizing oneself, by listening to the infinite in oneself. This is the dialogue with the inner voice, the "silent, thin voice" [1 Kings 19:13]. As this dialogue opens beyond awareness (fear) of God into love, exile ends.

The higher return home is a state of love, the return to God as His always loved one. This transcendent, ecstatic experience is usually prepared by the lower return but the experience of infinite love may occur first and inspire the return to oneself. Nevertheless, the depth and the duration of the gift of the higher *tshuvah* depends upon the lower: that there be a real person.

Hiding and Seeking

In the Song of Songs, the Bride seeks "whom my soul loves":

> I opened to my beloved; but my beloved had turned away, and was gone: my soul failed when he spoke: I sought him, but I could not find him; I called him, but he gave no answer. . . . [5:5]

From the human point of view, God hides. From God's point of view, He is always seeking and man hides;[8] He is always there (there is nothing else), and man need only open his eyes. In the *Midrash*, God and man "argue" over who should take the initiative in returning to each other:[9]

The Congregation of Israel said to the Holy One, "It is up to you", as it is said [Lam. 5:21]: "Return us, O God, to You, and [then] we shall return". But God said back to Israel, "It is up to you", as it is said [Zach. 1:3]: "Return to Me, and [then] I shall return to you, says the Lord of Hosts."

The reward for seeking is finding God. The measure of the pleasure and profound happiness in a person's life is the depth to which he has experienced the Infinite. The period of this "reward" has no limit, a man's soul continues to derive its supreme pleasure for eternity. Not finding God is its own punishment. As the kabbalist Rabbi Chaim Luzzatto explains:[10]

Man is the creature created for the purpose of experiencing God. . . . This is all that God desires of man, and it is the entire purpose of His creation. . . . Every fault (*chisaron*; lacking) is merely the absence of God and the concealment of His presence. The closeness of God and the illumination of His presence is therefore the root and cause of every perfection that exists.

On the personal level, God is always to be found. He hovers as an eagle hovers over her young [Deut. 32:11], "touching and not touching". Were God to either fully reveal his presence (allow himself to be completely found), or cease his continuous recreation of the world, existence would instantaneously vanish. "Touching and not touching" from above is reflected in man's "running and returning" from below. Thus Ezekiel's vision of the divine Chariot [1:14], in which ". . . the living creatures (*chayot*) run and return like the appearance of lightning", is interpreted to refer to the life force (*chai'ut*). As is breathing in and breathing out, the running and returning of *tshuvah* is the pulsation of the life force itself.

In relation to the *sefirot*, the return "home" is to *Binah* (Understanding), the Higher Mother, whose inner attribute is happiness. Happiness (*simchah*) is the inner life force associated with the female.[11] In the mind, one becomes happy because a profound understanding is experienced as a "returning home", as a truth one has always known. What was darkness (non-awareness) becomes illuminated by the insight from *Chochmah* (Wisdom, the Higher Father).[12] This illumination is a new insight of unity. The process of understanding is the *relating* of an idea (or a person's life, or a given situation) to the infinite, or at least, to a higher order of unity. The deeper the understanding, the more the unity of all reality is understood. The Talmud states: "Who is a wise man? One who sees what will be born". This has been interpreted to mean, the one who sees how each aspect of reality is brought into being from the *ayin*, from absolute nothingness.[13]

Tshuvah is the inner dynamic. The "outer" dynamic is equanimity (*hish 'tavut*; from the Hebrew root meaning "equal"). This is God's way of relating to the Creation, the perspective from eternity. Equanimity is not considered a form of pious passivity but rather the expression of an almost inhuman commitment. The achievement of equanimity in a person's daily life is strongly connected to the practice of the *mitzvot l'shmah*; that is, without ego attachment to the result (see Ch. III, sect. 2). Thus the Talmud states that there is no reward for a *mitzvah* in this world. The practice of the *mitzvot* without attachment is an expression of equanimity, an expression of absolute trust in God's love.

Equanimity is the psychic analogue to the transcendent light of Infinity which encompasses every point in reality equally.[14] In contrast, the immanent light of Infinity embodies the aspiring "run and return" of *tshuvah*. The inner circle of *tshuvah* exists within the outer "static" or meditative circle of a person's equanimity towards daily life. This is an interpretation of the phrase in the vision of Ezekiel [1:17]: ". . . the wheel within the wheel". In Kabbalah, it is explained that the Hebrew letters *samech* [O] and final *mem*, express two levels of consciousness. The *mem* is called the Coming World (*olam ha'ba*), the state of pure being (*shalom*), the state of the Garden (See Ch. VI, sect. 4). The *samech* is called the Future to Come (*l'atid l'vo*), the state of messianic or fifth dimensional consciousness—a higher revelation than the World to Come. According to one Kabbalistic tradition, the wedding ring placed by the groom on the index finger of the right hand of the bride is in the form of a circle within a square: ⊡—the *samech* within the final *mem*: fifth dimensional consciousness within the fourth; the Messiah within the Garden.[15]

3. The Destined Woman

Sometimes a man will merely glance at a certain woman and the experience can be so emotionally violent that he realizes she is from his true life, that his ordinary life has been a lie. In Yiddish, she is called his *b'shert* (in Hebrew, *bat zug*), his predestined soul mate. Desire for the *b'shert* has its origin in the primordial moment of the creation of souls. In essence, this is the most fundamental desire, *the desire within sexual desire*: the drive to return to absolute being. One who recognizes his *b'shert* (or a spark from her soul in another woman), even for a moment,[16] feels its irresistible demand. (The Sages say that when King David saw a small portion of Abigail's leg for one instant,[17] the light of the experience carried him a distance of three miles.)[18] All other considerations, even life and death, are nullified in its intensity, in its possibility. The force that demands to break out is the "raw", dark life being held back. The *ayin* within the psyche, the messianic force.[19]

The desire for the Messiah is the desire to end existence. The Sages speak of the wars and destruction which will precede or accompany the coming of the Messiah, of the "birth pangs of the Messiah". All values and all authority opposing the messianic force are destroyed by its intensity. Only the vessel of pure consciousness (*shalom*) can receive the Messiah. If the messianic force breaks into a world, or into a mind which has not achieved clarity, that vessel shatters. The tragic fate of false or premature messianic movements such as the Bar Kochba Revolt, Shabbtai Tzvi, and Jacob Frank bear witness to their tremendous destructive potential. This fear explains the stance of certain religious groups who resist "forcing the hand of the Messiah" by what they consider to be precipitous acts, such as the establishment of the secular State of Israel.

The lineage of Messiah (the House of David) passes through a strange series of sexual relations and through Jewish and non-Jewish ancestors. Starting with Adam and Eve, the messianic line evolved through the incestuous relations of Lot's daughters with their father; Judah and Tamar (his daughter-in-law who disguised herself as a prostitute); Boaz and Ruth, the Moabite proselyte woman; Jesse and his wife (whom he thought was his concubine at the time of conception); and David and Batsheva. These unions will be consummated by the *Shabbat* union between the Messiah and his *b'shert*. The Talmud says that Batsheva, the *b'shert* of King David, was ready for him from the six days of creation but that David "ate her raw".[20] He arranged that her husband Uriah be killed in battle in order to take her for himself. According to the *Midrash*, their first son, who died nameless before he was circumcised, was the Messiah.

Against the experience of the *b'shert*, or of other traces of the revelation of the Messiah, ordinary reality will react to preserve and to avenge itself. The *Midrash* says that Adam and Eve had sexual relations on the sixth day, whereas they should have waited until *Shabbat* which represented a higher spiritual level. But when Adam saw Eve, his desire was too great. Rashi quotes the opinion that they had intercourse, and that when the snake saw them, he became jealous. The snake (who is called *satan*) is the other side of the Messiah ("snake" in *gematria* equals "Messiah").[21] The snake's jealousy is the negative power of the day to day—the intense demands by close ones, the sudden appearance of compelling circumstances and obstacles.[22] Circumstances and obstacles express the force of ordinary reality fighting for its own life. Everyday life has its "ego" which resists nullification as the human ego resists. Yet in everyday life, as in nature itself, there exists the drive to return. The revenge taken by circumstances against the experience of the *b'shert* or other instances of messianic consciousness could be understood in another way. Not as a striking back but as life in exile struggling to return to its own origin, rushing into the experience of the *ayin* and "eating it raw". Thus the Talmud speaks of the Messiah as the son who is constantly aborted.[23]

The nullification of ordinary reality is related to the essence of *Shabbat*. The perfect state of *Shabbat* is *shalom* (peace, unity). On *Shabbat* creativity ceases, struggle ceases. Jewish law identifies such creativity in accordance with the thirty-nine categories of activities involved in the building of the Tabernacle,[24] the symbol for the very purpose of existence. Likewise for the individual, the work that ceases is one's life work. *Shabbat* expresses the transformation from the six workdays of purposeful existence to "rest". One rests in one's home within time,[25] the pure beingness that is symbolized by God's "rest". As the *Shabbat* (the guarded, enclosed Garden) *intensifies*, one "tastes" its inner pleasure, the pleasure within time.[26] The *Shabbat* is the bride of Israel in the kabbalistic song ("*Lecha Dodi*") that all sing in welcoming the *Shabbat* on Friday evening:

> Come, my Beloved, to meet the Bride;
> to welcome the face of *Shabbat* . . .
>
> for she is the source of blessing;
> from the primordial beginning,
> she was chosen . . .

NOTES

1. See Ch. V, sect. 2: Reincarnation. It is one of the tenets of Jewish faith that the resurrection of the body will take place in the final stage of the Messianic period. Maimonides, *Mishnah Torah*, Sanhedrin, Ch. 10.

2. Rav A. I. Kook, *Orot HaKodesh*; Ibid., p. 21.

3. Time is the first and most subtle form or "womb" in human consciousness. Time is related to the *sefirah* of *Binah*, the Higher Mother. In the *Etz Chaim*, the initial Mother in Kabbalah is called Mehitabel, the wife of Hadar, the last of the primordial "Kings of Edom" [Gen. 36]. Her name equals in *gematria zman*, "time" (See Ch. II, n. 16 on *Gematria*).

4. *Sefer Bahir* 31.

5. It is taught in Chassidism that there are three levels of exile of the *Shechinah*: the exile of Israel among the nations; more deeply, the exile of Israel in Israel; and most deeply, the exile of man from the divine spark in himself.

"Egypt" (*mitzraim*), means straits or confinements. "All exiles are called by the name Egypt . . ." [*Vayikra Rabbah* 13:4].

6. The term *ba'al tshuvah* (one who returns to the practice of Judaism) is often

misleadingly translated as "penitent". Although there is a genuine element of regret for past mistakes in the process of return, there is little idea of puritanical guilt or self-laceration which the term conjures up. In fact, a person overcome with guilt or sadness cannot make *tshuvah*. As Rabbi Nachman says, "Depression causes one to forget His Name".

7. As taught by Rabbi Pinchas of Koretz in relation to the tendency to "lie" (any manifestation of disharmony), it takes twenty-one years of spiritual labor to uproot and rectify an innate negative character trait. The first seven years rectifies its associated habits and false actions, the second seven years rectifies its impact on the emotions, and the final seven rectifies the mind. And the Sages teach that even with this effort, success requires God's help. Steinsaltz, *The Long Shorter Way*; Ibid., p. 38.

8. There is an anecdote concerning the young grandson of a famous rabbi who, while playing hide-and-seek, hid himself from the other children. The little boy ran weeping to the rabbi: "Grandfather, I hid myself and no one looked for me!" Whereupon the rabbi was deeply moved and answered, "Why, that is the very same thing that God is saying all the time". Ibid., p. 144.

9. *Midrash Shochar Tov, Tehillim* 85 (using different quotes). See also *Sanhedrin* 97b.

10. *The Way of God* (Feldheim, 1981), pp. 41, 45, 241.

11. The basic mystical sound associated with the state of returning in happiness is the 30th of the 72 Divine Names: *Om*—which derives from the *im*, Mother. *Om* appears in the Torah in the expression *home libi*: the sound or utterance coming from the vibration of the heart. It is also related to warmth (*chom*)—all are of the Mother. *Shalom* (peace) contains the sound-root *om*.

The Divine Name *Om* equals *bitul*—selflessness, self-negation, destruction of the ego. *Shalom* can be read *"shel om"*—of peace, possessing the property of, or derived from, *om*. *Shalom* is the possession of *om*, which is self-negation. Thus peace depends upon the internal process of *bitul*.

12. The mind is likened to earth which must be constantly cultivated. Ploughing the mind is known as "the deep meditation of *Ima* (Mother)". The lower earth is ploughed by action (*mitzvot*). Fruits of the unploughed field are the mind's fantasies which are infertile.

13. *Tamid* 32a. See *Tanya*, Ch. 43.

14. See Overview, sect. 1: The Creation, and the *Tzimtzum*.

15. See further on this point, Rav Y. Ginsburgh, *The Alef-Beit in Jewish Thought* (Aronson, 1991), pp. 227-228.

16. In the doctrine of reincarnation, sparks from the soul of the *b'shert* can exist in another woman or man. See Ch. V, n. 19., for a description of how this may manifest.

17. Abigail, Mical, as well as Batsheva (the three wives of David), were David's *b'shert* or contained sparks from her soul.

18. *Megillah* 14b.

19. In the realm of action, the leap of Nachshon ben Amidav, Prince of the

Tribe of Judah (the tribe of David and of the Messiah) expresses the messianic act. According to the *Midrash*, Nachshon jumped straight into the Red Sea when the Israelites were trapped by the Egyptians. He continued even as the sea reached his throat. His leap into faith (the night sea) opened the miracle of the messianic dimension. According to Rashi, at that moment, all the waters in the world opened.

20. *Sanhedrin* 107a; *Zohar* I, 73b.

21. See Ch. II, n. 16, on *Gematria*.

22. On the practical level, this type of resistance is known during the last hours before *Shabbat* (which is considered 1/60th of the World to Come; *Berachot* 57b). Those who have attempted to emigrate to the Land of Israel (which is on the level of *Shabbat*) have often had to overcome unexpectedly intense resistance from family and friends, and have often had to reject new and attractive opportunities.

23. *Sanhedrin* 96b.

24. *Shabbat* 7:2.

25. According to Kabbalah, as *Shabbat* approaches all created Worlds begin to ascend, each World to that above, to an altogether higher spiritual-energy level. *Pri Etz Chaim*, Intro. to *Sha'ar HaShabbat*. See Overview, sect. 4: Breaking of the Vessels.

The cycle of the six days of creation followed by the seventh day of *Shabbat* on which God "rested" is seen as the basic cycle inherent in Creation. The cycle of the seven days repeats itself continually in the cycles of seven years, of seven sabbatical years (*Jubilee*), and of seven millenia.

26. According to *Halachah*, the evening of *Shabbat* (Friday evening) is the most propitious and traditional night for a scholar and his wife to have conjugal relations. In terms of the *sefirot*, *Shabbat* is the union of *Malchut* with *Tiferet*. See also A. Hershel, *The Shabbat* (New York, 1961).

Chapter V

Passage Through the Generations

1. Memory

The Jewish psyche is the expression of a consistent spiritual experience over 150 generations. (The revelation of monotheism to Abraham was 3800 years ago [c. 1812 B.C.E.]). Although Jews have lived in physical subservience, Jewish consciousness itself has never yielded to a foreign spirituality.[1] The Jewish people differ from other ancient peoples such as the Chinese, for example, who have undergone radical transformations spanning from their original paganism, through Taoism, Confucianism, Buddhism, Shintoism, Christianity, and perhaps Communistic atheism—and remained Chinese. Throughout Jewish history, when a person ceased to identify with the Jewish religion, he commonly ceased being a member of the community and assimilated into the dominant culture.[2] As a result, each Jew today is born into a family with ancient roots—a family which has managed not only to survive physically but has chosen and rechosen its Jewish identity over the generations. It is a tragic fact that the history of every family includes martyrs who died in order to affirm their Jewishness. Thus it would be expected that the Jewish psyche is profoundly affected by inherited structures and proclivities that constitute its unique collective subconscious.[3]

A person actively participating in the Jewish tradition experiences reality through a collective memory, memory passed through the generations by the reliving of primordial rituals and experiences. Moses's commandment to the Jewish people has been honored: "You shall not forget the things that you saw with your own eyes . . . and you shall make them known to your children and to your childrens' children" [Deut. 4:9]. As sophisticated as he may be, a Jew is also a "primitive"; his consciousness is both modern and archaic. His memory is his re-enacting, his *re-being*. It is not a remembering of things past. All of the festivals are remembered and *happen* every year. His Torah is the same, his language, his land, his archetypal enemies, his people are the same difficult people. The memory of Israel is

45

founded in the written and oral Torah which has been interpreted and re-interpreted, commented upon with commentaries upon commentaries. So that the mind of each generation is in the next, the views of each generation are reconciled with the next; so that the ongoing revelation is never interrupted.

Meaningful continuity depends not only on the connection to the ancestral mind but also to the ancestral purpose. Dedication to God's purpose—to be a holy nation, to be God's instrument—is what is implied by the concept of the chosen people. According to the *Midrash*, the concept of Israel existed before the universe was created. The Talmud relates that the opportunity to fill the role of Israel was first offered to and rejected by the nations of the world until the "yoke of the Torah and *mitzvot*" was accepted by the Jewish people at Mt. Sinai, sight unseen (*na'ase v'nishma*).[4] In the resultant triangular covenant between God, Israel, and the Torah, God promised that He will remain concerned with the world and with the Jewish people and thus guarantee that existence has meaning. More specifically, there are three guarantees made by God to Israel through the covenant of the Torah: (a) that Israel will never be totally annihilated;[5] (b) that the Torah will never be cut off from Israel's seed;[6] and (c) that Israel will ultimately return to the Land of Israel.[7] In return, Israel agreed that no matter what happens to her she will affirm God's unity and goodness, and will work for the realization of the total possibility of being, and for the ultimate perfection of the Creation.

Continuity requires that the modern state of Israel continue the purpose of Abraham's family, of the Tribes in Sinai, of ancient Israel, and of Israel in Exile. In this way, the Jewish people "sit with the Elders of the Earth" [Prov. 31:23].[8] "Sitting together" is the essence of archaic consciousness; the reliving of experience through Torah, *mitzvot*, festivals, and through sharing and resharing the meaning of those experiences. But it is also planning for the future, planning how Israel is to become Israel. And it is also seeking with the elders among the nations the way man is to become man, how the unity of Adam's soul is to be restored. At this level, Jewish consciousness reaches full potentiality, the level of great-mindedness.

Recurrence and the reliving of experience are essential elements in what is meant by meaning. The memory relived in all the Torah festivals is of the exodus from an Egypt deeper than history: the coming out from slavery into freedom, from unconsciousness into consciousness.[9] Passover begins in the memory of Egyptian slavery; Purim in the Babylonian captivity; Chanukah in the occupation and religious oppression of the Greeks; *Tisha B'Av*[10] in the Babylonian destruction of the First Temple, and in the Roman destruction of the Second Temple. Archetypal events are seen to recur: the Roman massacres and the destruction of Jerusalem recur in the Holocaust; the Exodus recurs in the waves of Soviet and Ethiopian Jewry returning to Israel; Babylon recurs in cities such as New York and Paris which the Jews again refuse to leave.

An eternal recurrence (the revolving circle) defies the idea of progress, and therefore, of purpose. The Jewish understanding of time incorporates both the moon (cyclic consciousness) and the sun (conventional historical consciousness). Jews return home to the archaic or "moon" dimension of consciousness:[11] the world of its great ancestors, of sacred journeys, of revelation, of the holy land, of the sacred Temple, of exile and return. But this journey of return is into the future, in the shape of a spiral, of which the birth of messianic consciousness is the final cycle.

Memory reaches back through the evolution or emanation of the physical forms of creation, through the Worlds and levels of soul, to the point of infinity from which consciousness evolves. The soul remembers or senses its primordial oneness with God from the time before the Creation. Thus the process of memory is analogous to the process of coming to consciousness. (Forgetting is not the loss of memories but the inability to retrieve them).[12] The infinite potential of memory, and a hint as to the primal experiences or "impressions" which remain in the subconscious, are given in the story of the "Seven Beggars" by Rabbi Nachman. There the blind beggar tells of the earliest memory of each of the "survivors" (the souls of *tzadikim*) of a "shipwreck" (death):

The first beggar remembered when they cut the apple from the branch (the cutting of the navel cord);

the second, when the lamp was lit (within his mother's womb);

the third, when the fruit began to form;

the fourth, when the seed was brought to plant the fruit;

the fifth, when the wise man invented the seed (the seed in the father's brain);

the sixth, the fruit's taste before it entered the fruit (the lowest level of soul; *nefesh* , *Malchut*);

the seventh, the fragrance before it entered the fruit (the next level of soul; *ruach*; *Zeir Anpin*);

the eighth, the appearance before it was on the fruit (the level of *neshamah*, *Binah*);

the ninth, the *blind* beggar remembered nothing (in Yiddish, *gor nisht*)—the *ayin* itself.[13]

2. Reincarnation (Gilgulim)

The Universal Soul of Adam

According to the Kabbalah, all of the souls of man were contained in the primordial soul of Adam which shattered in the Fall. The purpose of reincarnation (*gilgulim*, from the Hebrew root meaning wheels) is to restore Adam's soul or mystical body, the parts of which are now scattered throughout humanity. Adam's soul divided into root souls which in turn broke into many "sparks". Each spark alone can serve as a soul in a human body but it is also possible that a person contains several sparks belonging to the same or even differing roots. The souls of the Jewish people devolve from the root souls of the three patriarchs, who divided into the twelve sons of Jacob, and then into the seventy who went down into Egypt as Jacob's household. These emerged from the womb of Egypt as the 600,000 souls who stood at Sinai. These 600,000 root souls are reincarnated as the Jewish people in each generation, the sparks of which are the souls of all the Jews alive today.[14]

The unique psychic structure of each individual is determined by the degree that one or several of the archetypes are influential. (These basic archetypes also relate to the sefirotic structure of the psyche.)[15] The patriarchs and their wives are the innate roots of the basic emotions: Love (Abraham-Sarah, *Chesed*); Fear or awe (Isaac-Rebecca, *Gevurah*); and Compassion (Jacob-Leah and Rachel, *Tiferet*). Each of the archetypes is also the root of the power to *rectify* that aspect of consciousness. Extending from the patriarchs and matriarchs are other great souls such as David, Hannah, Deborah, Rabbi Akiva, etc., which in turn extend their roots into contemporary Jewish families. A soul is not simply reincarnated over and over again. As Rabbi Nachman said, God does not do the same thing twice. Every person born expresses a new potential.

Kabbalah teaches that the mission of Israel in respect to Adam's universal soul pertains to the rectification of consciousness. This mission involves the restoration of the consciousness which existed in the Garden before the Fall, and then beyond that state to messianic consciousness. (Adam's level of consciousness [pure being or *shalom*] did not prevent the Fall; See Ch. VI, sects. 3 and 4.) The role of Israel is to withstand the idols and "lies" of the world by standing as witness to the absolute unity of all existence with God. (This power is the positive side of Israel's "stiff-neckness".) The will-power of Israel is associated with the *sefirah* of *Da'at* (knowledge) which expresses the fundamental unification of opposites (*Chochmah-Binah*). (Its first usage in the Torah is in reference to the sexual relation between Adam and Eve: "And Adam knew [*ya'dah*] Eve his wife" [Gen. 4:1].) Israel's struggle can be understood as rebuilding the inner strength in Adam's soul to withstand and to overcome the dominance of the snake's power, the power of doubt (the first separation) which eventually leads to the fragmentation of consciousness. But the power to redeem reality as a whole appears to be beyond Israel. The *Zohar* holds that redemption will come about through God's miraculous intervention and not solely through human effort.[16] Thus Israel strives but does not triumph, although individuals may triumph, if only in moments.

Passage Through the Generations

Reincarnation represents the passage of souls through the generations: "A generation goes and [the same] generation comes" [Eccles. 1:4].[17] The immortal soul is on an independent journey but cannot act without its inherited physical "garment", which includes mental capacity, character traits, and a body. It is the soul's "garment" which suffers death.[18] The passage of the Jewish soul involves the process of rectification through the fulfilling of *mitzvot* either not undertaken in previous lives, improperly performed, or transgressed. For example, a person may be reborn as a *cohen* (priest) in order to fulfill specific *mitzvot* associated with cohenim, which in turn, are related to the perfection of specific aspects of the soul.

The character of judgment that often applies in the process of reincarnation and in the Torah generally is "poetic justice" or "measure for measure."[19] Thus the *Ari* teaches that people who have committed certain types of transgressions may be reincarnated as animals,[20] or be "locked up" in inanimate or mute objects such as a stones, etc.[21] (In contrast, the judgment of nature is strictly cause and effect). The process of reincarnation also serves as an approach to the understanding of innocent suffering. In the writings of the *Ari*, for example, Job's fate is understood to involve the rectification of the reincarnated soul of Terah, the pagan father of Abraham. According to this view, the understanding of the nature and justice of a specific person's suffering must span more than one lifetime.

Although there are innumerable aspects and manifestations in respect to each *mitzvah*, the process of rectification often involves those *mitzvot* relating to human relationships from previous lives. There are three primary types of relationships in this regard: parent-child, master-disciple, and husband-wife. Strictly speaking, only men are required to be reincarnated. Likewise, the *mitzvah* of procreation (*pru v'ru*) applies only to men. Both physical and spiritual procreation is solely a male *obligation*. The female soul is considered whole and self-contained as compared to the dynamic (necessarily incomplete) nature of the male soul. The female soul re-enters the cycle "in order to be found" by her soul's mate. The *b'shert* is the daughter, sister, and mother of the male; and he is the father, brother, and son of her soul—rather, of their one soul. A woman agrees to re-enter and to suffer in the cycle of reincarnation for the sake of the man; that is, in order to help him fulfill his soul's destiny in each life. Her devotion is to her husband's highest essence or essential self. Eve was created as a "help against" Adam (*ezer k'negdo*; Gen. 19). This is interpreted to mean that a wife helps her husband to be his highest self; otherwise, she is against him.[22]

There are two basic attitudes regarding the emphasis to be given to reincarnation. Some view the doctrine of reincarnation as revealing the deeper dimensions of the process of *tikkun* working through history and Torah. In this respect, for example, the figures of Moses and Jethro are understood to be the reincarnations of Abel and Cain, and therefore involved in their rectification. Likewise, David, Batsheval and Uriah are seen as the reincarnation of Adam, Eve, and the Snake, etc. Chassidism would generally discourage a person's seeking to explore his own past lives. This is so because one must experience the existential freedom of the present in order to rectify blemishes inherent in past impressions on the psyche. The dangers of self-deception are great; the doctrine which reveals the working of reincarnation is extremely complicated. Thus even the *Ari* taught that this knowledge is not accessible without a Master.[23]

Nevertheless, the view of the *Ari* is that knowledge of the root of one's soul and of past lives is necessary in order to fully understand oneself and one's purpose. If one fails to fulfill that function one is literally wasting one's life. The inner voice guides a person towards his *tikkun*, as do his talents, special interests, and even compulsive inclinations. It is also taught that *mitzvot* which are easy for a person to perform may indicate that they have been mastered in previous reincarnations. On the other hand, those *mitzvot* which are difficult or which offer the most resistance point to the direction of rectification. One cannot know what the destined act is until one meets it. "Every man has his hour" [Sayings of the Fathers, 4:3] is interpreted to mean that a man's whole life may be directed to "one hour", one event, one meeting.[24]

A phenomenon related to reincarnation is *ibbur* (impregnation). *Ibbur* refers to the temporary indwelling of a soul spark from a *tzaddik* or another deceased person in order to achieve a specific purpose. The *ibbur* usually enters a worthy man who is aspiring to fulfill a specific *mitzvah* but who lacks the ability to achieve it. If the *tzaddik* had an affinity to that task,[25] a spark of his soul may indwell in the person, remaining until that task is accomplished, until the "host" soul commits some damaging act or sin, or until death.[26] When a person becomes unusually empowered and committed towards a task or life goal, something quite extraordinary in respect to his previous life history, it may be considered a sign of an *ibbur*. He may suddenly realize that he has grown in stature and conviction, or that he is able to see and experience things that were previously beyond his powers. Literally, he becomes a greater man, a man who has gone beyond himself.

In the view of Kabbalah, therefore, a person is never just himself. A person's life is never just a life. Each person is born with a unique goal to achieve which affects humanity and its future. The Sages teach that each infant born contains a spark of the Messiah; that with each new child humanity advances. This understanding also underlies the injunction that the saving of lives (*pikuach nefesh*) overrides the other *mitzvot*.[27] Because birth is the gate through which souls enter to fulfill the potential of existence, "To be fruitful and multiply" was the first Torah directive given to man [Gen. 1:28], and is called the "great *mitzvah*".

NOTES

1. A clear example is that of the Ethiopian Jews who were cut off from the mainstream of Jewish life for over two thousand years, and who thought of themselves as the only Jews left in the world. For example, they do not have the holiday of Chanukah which commemorates events in the 2nd century B.C.E. By tradition, they trace their ancestry to King Solomon and the Queen of Sheba.

2. Jewish law, on the other hand, holds that anyone born of a Jewish mother remains a Jew despite the fact that the mother or her children may have converted to another religion.

Instead of numbering in the hundreds of millions as would be expected of a people who have kept their identity over such a long historical period, there are only 14,000,000 (the "remnant").

3. Many kabbalists view proselytes as returning Jewish souls (See *Etz Chaim*, *Shaar* 49, Ch. 3; *Shaar* 50, Ch. 7). Nevertheless converts to Judaism receive a new soul from the root of Abraham or Sarah. Thus they often take the name *Avraham ben Avraham* (Abraham, the son of Abraham) or *Sarah bat Sarah* (Sarah, the daughter

of Sarah). In this way, they are heir to the total collective subconscious of the Jewish people.

4. Even at this point, however, the Talmud relates that God actually forced Israel to accept by threatening to crush them with the mountain if they refused. "He suspended the mountain over them as a barrel" [*Shabbat* 88a]. It was only at the time of Purim during the Babylonian Exile that both the written and oral Torah were finally accepted by free choice.

5. *Tamchuma Etchanan* 1.

6. *Shir Hashirim Rabba* 1:13.

7. *Zohar*, Vol. II, 16a; *Pesikta Rabbati* 32.

8. As taught by Rabbi Hillel of Paritch on *Shir HaShirim*. Ordination of rabbis from master to disciple began with Moses and continued until the 4th century C.E., when as a result of the Roman persecutions in Israel, the chain was broken. The Sages of Safed in the 16th century tried to revive this ancient practice but were not successful. Maimonides has written that ordination (*samichah*) would have to be re-established before the coming of the Messiah [*Mishah Torah, Sanhedrin* 1:3].

9. It is taught in Chassidism that: "In every generation *and everyday* a person is obliged to regard himself as if he had that day come out of Egypt". The text is from the *Mishnah* [*Pesachim* 10:5], except that the words "and everyday" have been added to emphasize the daily recurrence of the event [*Tanya*, Ch. 47]. There the Exodus is connected to the daily saying of the *Shema* prayer: "The Lord is our God, the Lord is One." That is, through the acceptance of the *Shema*, the soul is released from the body and is absorbed in God's unity—the spiritual form of the Exodus from Egypt.

10. *Tisha b'Av* (the 9th day of the Hebrew month of *Av* which occurs at the end of summer, the hottest and most desolate part of the year) is also by tradition the date of the capture of Bethar, the last stronghold of the Bar Kokhba rebellion (135 C.E.), and the building of a pagan temple on the site of the Temple (136 C.E.). This line of catastrophes is linked to the recurrence of punishment for the sin of the "spies" who spoke against entering the Land of Israel from the wilderness of Sinai on that day [Num. 14], and to the subsequent decree by God that that generation would not enter the Land of Israel.

11. In the blessing of the moon, the symbol of resurrection and of Israel, and especially of the Kingdom of David, one affirms three times: "David King of Israel is alive and exists".

The idea of the "end enwedged into the beginning" (See Ch. IV, sect. 2) is expressed in certain of the holidays. *Tisha b'Av*, the lowest point in the cycle of the Jewish year, is also potentially the highest day—the day when the soul of the Messiah was born in Heaven [*Intro. Ester Rabba* 11; *Yerushalmi, Berachot* 2:4].

12. Evidence is beginning to appear that the cortex of the brain stores a permanent record of every experience. Recent studies related to the Savant Syndrome in which certain retarded and handicapped individuals have displayed spectacular rote memory ("an island of brilliance in a sea of mental handicap") seem to support this conclusion. During surgery when the cortex has been stimulated, it is reported

that fully conscious patients under local anesthesia often ramble on in great detail about previously inaccessible incidents from their past. D. Treffert, *An Unlikely Virtuoso*, in The Sciences (Jan./Feb., 1988), pp. 28, 35.

13. It is told of the *Baal Shem Tov*, the grandfather of Rabbi Nachman, that he would ask each new disciple who came to him: *Wus Gednst Tu?* "What do you remember?"

In Rabbi Nachman's story, four levels of soul are recognized. Other systems articulate five levels, the fifth being *Yechida* corresponding to *Keter*. When four levels of soul are indicated, *Chochmah* expresses the *ayin* of Divine Nothingness. See Overview, n. 10, and sect. 2: The Five Worlds.

For an interpretation of the "Seven Beggars" and other tales of Rabbi Nachman drawn from the Bratzlav Chassidic sources, see A. Kaplan, *Rabbi Nachman's Stories* (Breslov Research Institute, 1983).

14. The complete manifestation or expression of the whole soul of Israel is 600,000 × 600,000 sparks or aspects [*Tanya*, Ch. 37].

15. Their essence as revealed by Kabbalah is as follows:

Patriarchic Archetypes of the Psyche

Isaac (fear; *Gevurah*)	Abraham (love; *Chesed*)

Jacob (compassion; *Tiferet*)

Aaron (sincerity; *Hod*)	Moses (trust; *Netzach*)

Joseph (truth; *Yesod*)

David (lowliness; *Malchut*)

In general, the matriarchs express the female dimension of the partriachic archetypes, although according to some systems, there are differences in this respect. The matriarchs are the spiritual or soul sources for space-consciousness, the patriarchs are the source of time-consciousness in the psyche.

The souls of the patriarchs and matriarchs express complex characteristics (each *sefirah* contains all of the other ten *sefirot* within itself; Figure 8, Overview). The connection to the primary characteristics or emotions associated with each of the patriarchs and matriarchs requires a deep understanding of their role in Torah.

16. *Zohar*, Vol. II, 9a; *Tikkunei Zohar*, Intro. 15a.

17. *Sefir Bahir* 155. It is said of Rabbi Nachman that he was a reincarnation of the soul of Simeon Bar Yochai who lived in the Roman period and was, according to tradition, the author of the *Zohar*.

18. Despite the importance of inheritance, there are many instances of a great soul being born to unworthy parents or in degrading circumstances. According to the *Ari*, certain exceptional souls cannot come into the world by any other means, being held, so to speak, in "capitivity" by the "other side". It is explained, for ex-

ample, that the soul of Rabbi Akiba, who came from a poor and simple family of proselytes, had to be born through such an inconspicuous channel to be "like unto Moses". Most clear in this respect is the line of the Messiah which involved problematic liaisons from its very inception. See Steinsaltz, *The Long Shorter Way*; Ibid.; pp. 9-12.

19. On reincarnation in general, see *Sefer HaGilgulim*. An idea of the complexity and the patterns involved in the process of reincarnation can be gained from the writing of Joseph Karo, the great Halachic authority and author of the authoritative *Shulchan Aruch* (Code of Jewish Law) in Safed during the 16th century. In the book *Maggid Meisharim*, which contains the teachings of his *Maggid* (teaching spirit or angel), the *Maggid* explains to Joseph Karo the secret of the reincarnation of his third wife:

> You must know that in her past [transmigration] this woman was a male, a virtuous rabbinic scholar but who was miserly—not spending on charity—and also stingy with his wisdom, refusing to teach others. Therefore he was . . . transmigrated into a female, measure for measure: he did not want to pour out blessing (material and spiritual) on others . . . therefore he is now incarnated in a female (embodying the receptive principle) . . . Therefore (your wife) . . . is very charitable (ie. unconsciously engaged in the *tikkun* of her soul), and also loves you because you spread Torah . . . Because these things are her *tikkun*, therefore she loves you. . . .
>
> Since she is a male soul she is not really your (predestined) mate . . . Because her soul is essentially a male soul (and so is yours), she could not produce offspring for you. If you object (and ask) how then could she bear children to her first husband, know that *his* soul contained female sparks; . . . And this is the reason for the delayed pregnancy of your wife, . . . and only now have female soul-sparks been added to her (soul) so that she can conceive for you. She merited this by doing good works and (for enduring suffering connected with you) . . .
>
> Behold, these sparks have now come to her from the soul of your (real, predestined) soul-mate. However, until now it was not possible . . . because she was married to another man and was widowed only now. By (your wife's) merits some sparks emanated from your real soul-mate to your (present) wife . . . and therefore she can (now) bear you children . . .

This quotation is from R. Werblowsky, *Joseph Karo* (JPS, 1980), pp. 112-114 where a fuller translation appears. This work also contains interesting details in respect to the lives of the Safed kabbalists.

20. According to the *Ari*, if a *tzaddik* is reincarnated in a non-human form, he is usually reincarnated as a fish. As eating is one of the primary means of the liberation of sparks captured in animals and plants, this is offered as one of the explanations as to why fish is a part of the traditional meal on *Shabbat*.

Similarly, there are stories in the writings of the *Ari* of oxen breaking into the *Beit Midrash* imploring and offering themselves to be slaughtered. These stories are also a reference to the ritual slaughter of animals in the time of the Temple, a process considered to liberate the sparks captured in the animals sacrificed. It was said that the animals became joyous when selected for sacrifice, and that no animal was sacrificed against its will.

21. See further, Overview, sect. 6: The Rectification of Reality, especially in relation to the rectification of nature.

22. See further in this regard, Ch. II, sect. 3: Male and Female Perception. The *Ari* further teaches that in the last generation prior to the coming of the Messiah (thought by many to be the present era), the people born will be the reincarnation of the generation that left Egypt [*Sha'ar Ha Gilgulim, Hakdama* 20]. That is, redemption will come based on the merit of women. In this generation, the women will dominate the men because they are free of the sin of the Golden Calf (the analogue of the Sin of Adam), having refused their husbands' demands to give up their jewelry to make the Golden Calf [*Sotah* 11b; *Shemot Rabbah* 1:12; *Bamidbar Rabba* 21:11; *Tanchuma, Pinchas* 7].

23. It is said of great *tzaddikim* that they see the root of a person's soul and his past lives. In response, people come or even write to their Rebbe to seek approval for proposed marriages, to seek help in the case of apparent barrenness, and to gain self-knowledge in respect to their *tikkun*. This tradition remains very strong in the Chabad tradition today which claims to number over one hundred *chassidim* all over the world.

24. See *Zohar*, Vol. II, 99b. A required *tikkun* may involve some context extraneous to one's true creativity. Or it may be, for example, that a top Talmudic mind devotes his life energy to the stock market, the ultimate goal of which is charity. The scenarios are endless and unknowable. Certainly it is often the case that financially successful businessmen focus their later life goals towards broader and more constructive activities; that is, towards *tikkun*. In the Jewish view, this is the only justification for devoting one's life to commercial activities.

25. For one of many examples, in the *Zohar* it is stated that the soul of Judah was present in the aged Boaz when he married Ruth and begat Obed, the grandfather of David (the line of the Messiah).

26. Conversely, the spark of the soul of an evil person who has just died is called a *dybbuk* (a spirit which must be exorcized). The *dybbuk* attaches itself to a person with whom it has an affinity. For example, the soul of a person who has been involved in sins connected with sexual relations might be drawn into a person who has an inner desire to commit those same acts.

27. There are three exceptions. See Ch. III, sect. 1: Dying for Truth.

Chapter VI

The Tzaddik's Mind

1. The Mind's Transparence

Of the 613 commandments of the Torah, there are six "continuous commandments" which define rectified consciousness; that is, total awareness of the infinite—the mind of the *tzaddik*.[1] These positive *mitzvot* (which have been likened to "cities of refuge")[2] apply to all persons, in all places, and at all times.[3] The fact that the Torah *commands* this state of mind implies that choosing is involved, that pure consciousness is potentially achievable by choices within the power of the ordinary man.

The first commandment of consciousness is trust in God: "I am the Lord your God, who has taken you out of the land of Egypt, from the house of slavery" [Exod. 20:2]. This is the first of the Ten Commandments. Although phrased as a statement, it is regarded as the commandment to have faith in the God of liberation. Simple faith (*emunnah pshuta*) is the most fundamental aspect of rectified consciousness because all others flow from it. It is the primary choice, and the continuing choice—the will to openness.[4] Faith is the infinite receptivity of the mind, the analogue in the psyche of the infinity of the physical universe. Faith, which is rooted in the highest level of *Keter* (the "Unknowable Head"), is blind because it can have no content or dogma, it is "dark" because it is pure potential, pure receptivity. Thus faith is the ultimate root of the female in each person, the innate "marriage" of the mind to the infinite.

Faith becomes *trust* as it is lived. Trust is active faith. In the structure being presented, trust is associated with the *sefirah* of *Netzach* (victory, eternity), the inner attribute of which is trust in the infinite.[5] Trusting God means trusting life, trusting the present. Living in the present is an expression of a person's inner security, which ultimately is dependent upon his faith in the meaning and in the immortality of life. One lives in the situation one finds oneself in; in fact, a person's *tikkun* in the spontaneous situation may *be* the preordained purpose of his life. Not to live in the present

56

Figure 1 **Rectified Consciousness**

The six commandments define a mental space which corresponds to the six directions of physical space, and to the six *midot* of the *sefirot*

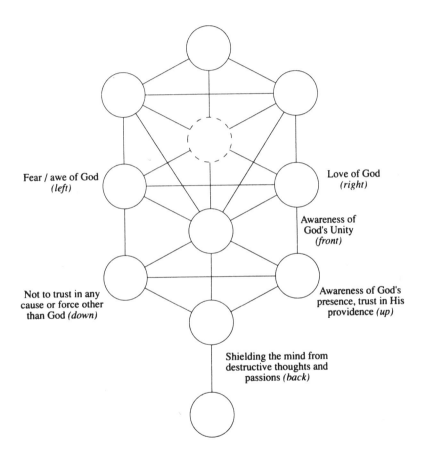

Fear / awe of God *(left)*

Love of God *(right)*

Awareness of God's Unity *(front)*

Not to trust in any cause or force other than God *(down)*

Awareness of God's presence, trust in His providence *(up)*

Shielding the mind from destructive thoughts and passions *(back)*

Figure 2 **Space-Model of Rectified Consciousness**

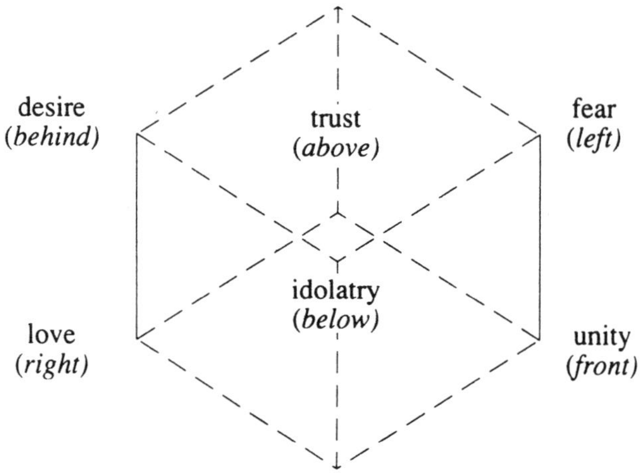

implies its own faith in the future: that one will live to reach the "future", and that one will receive more security and pleasure there.[6] By living in the present, everything is at stake. Everything being at stake forces one deeper and deeper into life, into the infinity in life.[7]

The second commandment of consciousness is to be free of idolatry: "You shall have no other gods before Me" [Exod. 20:3].[8] This is the second of the Ten Commandments. These two commandments are the only two heard directly from God (the other eight came through Moses), and as such, are the basic origins of Jewish consciousness. Not to have "other gods before Me" means not to put intermediaries between oneself and God[9]—whether they be other forms of god, nature, or idols such as wealth, positions of power, or beauty. The most powerful and subtle idol that stands before God is the ego. The *mitzvah* against idolatry is to see through everything, through everyone, and especially through oneself to the inner divinity. Not to "fall" for the world, not to idolize a part of the whole, not to idolize an experience or person. More precisely, it is the commandment to be in direct relation, to talk directly and personally with God. Not to be afraid or to feel unworthy, not to place any psychological barriers before Him.

Not to "fall" for the world does not mean not enjoying the world. A person is forbidden to torture himself or his body with asceticism or penitence "that God has no desire for". The Sages say, "Are the Torah's prohibitions not enough for you that you create new prohibitions for yourself?"[10] Not only is a person forbidden to multiply prohibitions and restrictions, he should actively taste the world. The Talmud says that a person will be held accountable to the Presence for every good and permitted thing that he sees but does not taste. Every pleasure that is not forbidden is, in this sense, compulsory; to reject the pleasures and beauty of this world is to reject God's benevolence.[11]

The third commandment is expressed by the *Shema*, the basic affirmation of Israel: "Hear O Israel, the Lord is our God, the Lord is One" [Deut. 6:4].[12] This is the commandment to reach the realization of the absolute unity of God in the "inner eye of the heart" (*Tiferet*); the realization that nothing other than God exists. According to the *Ari*, the proper inner intention (*kavannah*) in reciting the *Shema* is the readiness to die at that very moment into God. The essence of the *Shema* is found in part of the yiddish song "*Dudele*" written by the chassidic master, R. Levi Yitzchak of Berditchev:

> Where can I find You (*du*)—
> And where can I not find You
>
> Above—You, Below—You
> to the East—You, to the West—You
> to the South—You, to the North—You
>
> if its good, its You;
> if its not—also You;
> It is You
> It is You

It is not only that all reality is God but that God is the most intimate self, "our" God. In effect, this is the commandment to mystical union.[13]

The fourth *mitzvah* is love of God: "And you shall love the Lord your God will all your heart, with all your soul, and with all of your might" [Deut. 6:5, which continues the prayer of the *Shema*]. It is taught that "with all your heart" means with both one's good and evil inclinations, that one can approach and even love God through one's lackings and passions. "With all your soul" is interpreted to mean "even at the expense of your soul", to the point of total self-sacrifice. "All your might" refers to the strength to love God with all one's possessions, and more fundamentally, in the face of the apparent evil He allows.

A person can love God to the degree that he is able to experience God's loving him. Love answers love "as in water, face answers to face" [Prov. 27:20]. Thus the Torah teaches, love God "for He is your life". When a person experiences the truth of the *Shema*, at that same moment, he knows love. And he spontaneously loves God because he experiences that he himself, and all souls, and all there is, is made of God's love. That "The whole earth is filled with His glory" (Isaiah 6:3). The *mitzvah* to love God is therefore essentially to praise, to arouse God's love. The deeper one's praise the less one's separate life exists.[14]

The fifth *mitzvah* of consciousness is to fear God: "You shall fear the Lord your God" [Deut. 6:13]. Fear in this context means awareness of divine providence. A person is to be aware that God is aware of him. Fear of God differs from simple fear of punishment in that the focus is not on the punishment but rather on the nature of the divine. "Fear of God" is a process of maturing, of realizing one's limitations and even helplessness. The higher fear is awe. Awe of God is the spiritual motion of running away or of withdrawing, the opposite movement from love. Thus the Sages teach "The left pushes away, while the right draws close".[15] Yet fear precedes love in mystical experience. That moment when one enters the dimension that is absolutely beyond the human is the moment of both fear and awe. As one approaches closer, awe may turn into shame for one's humanness.

A lover fears the loss of love. A person's love of God is like an intense new love, and as well, like the established love between a man and his wife of many years. But it is never secure. Once a person has known the infinite, he knows that the fear of God has love at its source. Fear of God becomes fear of being cut off; rather, of cutting oneself off because God is always there. It is the fear that one may call out and hear only one's inner deadness. At each new level the fear of lapsing into staleness, of becoming dead, stimulates deeper levels of aspiration. Fear dissolves the shells that constantly evolve around spiritual experience, no matter what level had been reached even the moment before. Thus fear and rebirth are related; fear shocks love into new life, new pulsation.

Love and fear are called the two "wings" of spiritual ascent. Fear or awe is the foundation of the *mitzvot*. The *Zohar* teaches that *mitzvot* performed without both love and fear lack the "wings" necessary to fly upward to Heaven; that is, they cannot unite everyday life with the infinite.[16] Fear without love leads to empty and habitual practice. Free, spontaneous love for God cannot establish channels into every aspect of life, day after day.

2. *The Other Side: Imagination, and the Unconscious*

The sixth commandment of consciousness is to guard one's mind from destructive thoughts and desires: "You shall not stray after your heart and after your eyes . . ." [Num. 15:39]. The Sages say that the heart represents thoughts of heresy; and the eyes, thoughts of "prostitution". According to the kabbalistic view, the experience of the flow of images through the mind is *Malchut* of *Binah*. The flow of clear consciousness (the life force of the Creation) enters the psyche through *Keter*. In *Binah*, the stream of consciousness fills with pictures ("letters of thought") which come to it from different areas in the psyche and from the environment. These "letters" or "seeds" are the ordinary static of the mind which have the potential to develop into fantasies, etc. (Sexual fantasy is "spilling the seed" in the mind.) "Lust", symbolizing all passions, is powered by these fantasies— leading to inevitable self-prostitution.

The structure and processes of the psyche are the analogues of primordial cosmic events such as the *Tzimtzum*, the Breaking of the Vessels, the emanation of the Five Worlds, etc. As these correspondences are understood, the structure of the unconscious and its creative power, the imagination, can be understood. The existence of destructive thoughts and images are the manifestation of the "broken vessels" which exist both in the unconscious (the "back brain"),[17] and in the culture which indeed heightens these images. The battle for the mind is for the content of its imagery; it is the battle for the person himself, who is where his mind is. The imagination is powered by the sexual drive, the basic drive. Thus, control of sexual desire expresses control of the unconscious, and *a fortiori*, of the total mind.[18] This is the basis for the *Zohar's* definition of the *tzaddik* as one who controls "the purity of the *brit*", and of the fact that the archetypal imagery of Kabbalah is sexual.

Both Kabbalah and the imaginative faculty are related to the *sefirah* of *Da'at* (Knowledge),[19] which expresses the *will* of the unconscious. According to the *Midrash*, God created worlds and destroyed them until He came to the possibility of this world.[20] Out of infinite potential He chose the reality which He then revealed in the Torah. God's "cosmic" act of self-limitation is the paradigm of the power of the human will to control the imagination. Rectified imagination is the union of wisdom (*Chochmah*) and prophecy (*Binah*), and is the broadest potential of the conscious mind. Improper imaginative associations, however, result in "adulteries" or perversions of meaning ("obscene" comparisons) which block or manipulate thought. Confused or perverse imagery may be the result of ignorance, or of a deliberate intention to restructure thought and values. This type of "cross circuitry" is used to achieve commercial and political goals, or to create the flash of an artistic effect. True associations or created images are, in effect, transparencies which reveal the infinity at their common core. Whenever a true image or link (*yichud*) is made, the individuality or "substances" of the two elements are cancelled out, just as the subjective personalities of a man and woman are obliterated in the ecstacy of union.

Consciousness is human light. Rectification involves transforming darkness to light, the unconscious to consciousness. The unconscious is related to the dark side of the moon, the "back" of consciousness. In the idiom of Kabbalah, the source of unconscious drives is traced to the primordial World of *Tohu* (Chaos), where each of the lower seven *sefirot* was a separate "king"; that is, expressed a particular psychic obsession (e.g., love [*Chesed*], "law and order" [*Gevurah*], art or physical beauty [*Tiferet*], sexuality [*Yesod*]. The "impressions" or drives represented by the seven destroyed "kings who reigned in the land of Edom"[21] remain part of the human unconscious and manifest as fantasies, psychological compulsions, or philosophic determinisms. Once recognized, however, these primal powers can be potentially integrated into a psychic whole and constructively guided by consciousness.

Although many of the fundamental working premises of psychoanalysis are rooted in Kabbalah (for example, the recognition of the unconscious, the centrality of the sexual drive, the attempt to heal by bringing repressed material into consciousness, etc.),[22] the Jewish view is that a person cannot be healed solely by his own or by other peoples' efforts. The essence of personal prayer, therefore, is for the self-knowledge and strength to control one's mind and heart; that is, for liberation from oneself in order to achieve God's will. The ability to conquer one's desires is, in fact, the primary definition of strength in Judaism. This is the dictum in *Sayings of the Fathers* [4:1]: "Who is mighty (*gibbor*), he who conquers his desire (*yetzer*)".

For those on the level of the *tzaddik*, it is possible, but nevertheless considered dangerous, to face sexual images and power fantasies in order "to elevate them to their root" in infinity. The *tzaddik* is often affected by "strange thoughts" originating in the minds of other people and in the general environment, especially during periods of prayer and meditation. When such a thought involves lust, for example, the *tzaddik* will dwell upon the fantasy, recognizing it as an image (a shell) "sucking" on a spark "fallen" from *Chesed* (love); if it involves a fantasy of violence, he will recognize it as fallen from *Gevurah* (fear/might); and if pride, as fallen from *Tiferet* (beauty). The *Baal Shem Tov* likened this process of *tik-kun* to a person counting his money (his prayer or meditation) while his children (the sparks of infinity) are held captive in these images and fantasies. The sparks come to him and say, "You have enough money. Ransom us!"[23] He will not merely push these thoughts out of his mind, or let them pass through. For the ordinary person, Judaism speaks of "guarding one's thoughts" or of "pretending to be deaf"; that is, of not dwelling on them, of not planning them to come true in reverie, etc. The *tzaddik* is obligated to "liberate" or "to elevate" these images by thinking them through to their inner root.

3. The Infinite Present

There is a seventh *mitzvah* which "strives" to be continuous, and this is prayer: "Would that one pray the whole day continuously" [*Y. Shabbat* 1:2]. According to some authorities, there is no commandment to pray in the Written Torah. Others say that the Torah prescribes prayer in times of trouble and anxiety, while yet others hold that the Written Torah obliges one to pray once a day. Rabbinic law has expanded the obligation to three times a day for men, and twice a day for women. In terms of the diagrammatic space model of consciousness presented in Figure 2 above, this commandment can be considered the point of self-consciousness at the center of the "cube". (In *Sefer Yitzirah*, the earliest extant book of Kabbalah, the universe is described as a cube expanding from a point.) Prayer is this conscious "I" or point. This seventh *mitzvah* corresponds to *Malchut*, the *sefirah* of self-consciousness, the expression in self of the totality of the other six *sefirot*.[24]

As a unity, the seven mitzvot of the mind express the essence of Jewish spiritual consciousness. The "direction" of each of the seven aspects is openness to the infinite. Consciousness clarifies as each aspect is intensified to its infinity. Each blemish of ego, however, is an intrusion of time (of mortality). In the transparent, timeless mind all seven dimensions are inter-included and unified.[25] They are "at peace" (*shalom*) in the present. As a person's total awareness clarifies through the process of inter-inclusion (transparency), he is drawn closer and closer to this state of pure being, the human analogue of God's recreating a new world every moment.[26]

4. Fifth Dimensional, and Messianic Consciousness

The rectification of the fourth dimension of time is the prerequisite for the revelation of the fifth dimension, the completely mystical dimension of the Messiah. The three spatial dimensions of consciousness discussed above correspond to: up-down, right-left, and front-back (Figures 1 and 2 above). The *Sefer Yitzirah* teaches that the fourth dimension is time (past-future), as defined by *Chochmah-Binah*. The fifth dimension is called soul or good-evil (i.e., "distance" from God) as defined by *Keter-Malchut*. (Abram was given the extra *hey* in his name [whose numerical value is 5] to make it Abra*h*am [Gen. 17:15], expressing the level of *yechida*, the fifth and highest level of soul.) In the rectified state of ordinary consciousness (*shalom*) discussed above, the universe is here and now. Fourth dimensional consciousness "adds" the dimension of the infinite beginning and infinite end to the eternal present. All of time is present simultaneously as consciousness expands towards (becomes aware of) both the past and future. As with the dimension of space in the physical universe, time is infinitely expanding mind.

Messianic consciousness is an expression of a quantum leap in intensity from fourth dimensional consciousness.[27] The total of the ten *mitzvot* of messianic or fifth dimensional consciousness[28] define the ultimate potential of the mind [Figure 3]. This is the level at which the divine spark of the soul interacts with the infinite in absolute unity—the mind of Messiah.

The achievement of the three highest aspects of consciousness, only briefly indicated below, is the inner meaning of the three historical stages of the "time of the Messiah": the historical coming of the Messiah (*Binah*), the building of the Third Temple (*Chochmah*), and the final Resurrection (*Keter*).[29] The first two of these aspects, which characterize fourth dimensional consciousness, nevertheless are considered part of the ultimate messianic process which culminates in the Resurrection. As will be discussed in Chapter VII, these two higher aspects of consciousness become active in mystical union or in the highest levels of meditation.

The eighth aspect or dimension of total consciousness is the *mitzvah* of return (*tshuvah*); the level of the higher return associated with the *sefirah* of *Binah* (See Ch. IV, sect. 2). At this level of consciousness, a person experiences the complete healing of his soul; of being "taken care of" to the core of his being—of continuously returning home to ever-deepening levels of awareness. Short of "seeing God's face"[30] there is no limit to *tshuvah*, no limit to the soul's capacity to experience God—which is its very purpose. This is what is meant by the *Zohar's* teaching that the "Messiah comes to make the *tzaddikim* do *tshuvah*".

The ninth dimension is the *mitzvah* of learning Torah, that every moment brings a new and constantly more sublime insight. It is taught that after the arrival of the Messiah, the Temple will be rebuilt. One of the

Figure 3 **Fourth Dimensional and Messianic Consciousness**

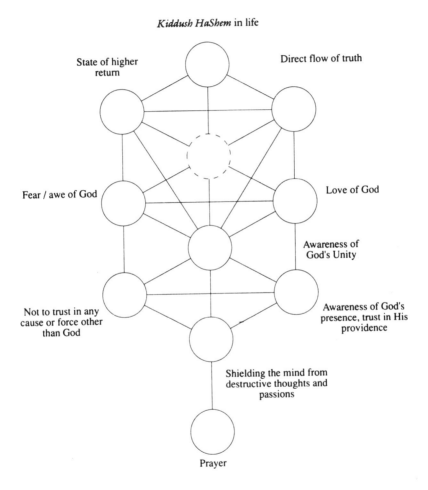

Kiddush HaShem in life

State of higher
return

Direct flow of truth

Fear / awe of God

Love of God

Awareness of
God's Unity

Not to trust in any
cause or force other
than God

Awareness of God's
presence, trust in His
providence

Shielding the mind from
destructive thoughts and
passions

Prayer

prophecies concerning the Temple is that ". . . a fountain will flow from the House of God" [Joel 4:18]. The flow of water (*Chochmah*) is a symbol for the wisdom of the Torah. This level of consciousness is the continuous experience of the revelation of Mt. Sinai in the mind.

The final messianic stage is the constant *mitzvah* of *Kiddush HaShem* in life, the *sefirah* of *Keter*. This dimension corresponds to the experience of dying in mystical union. One of the principles of Jewish belief is that after a certain period beyond the coming of the Messiah, the dead will be resurrected.[31] This is the only level of consciousness being described which is completely beyond human experience: that of continually dying in the "kiss" and being resurrected. In this final stage of the Creation, all reality will be reunited with God, not only the sparks but also the shells of physical reality. Having died—the unrectified, natural ego being finally "dead"—the soul will experience life as an eternal pulsation or oscillation of living/dying into God.

NOTES

1. By tradition, the *tzaddik* commands extraordinary powers, powers which express the microcosmic nature of consciousness. Rabbi Chaim Vital, the great student of the *Ari*, described some of the powers of his Master in the Introduction to *Sha'ar Hakdamot*: The *Ari* could read a person's face (primarily the letters on his forehead) and tell all that he had done and would do, including the root of his soul in the primordial soul of Adam, his past lives, etc. He knew the language of the birds and the trees, he could read the signs in the formations of the birds in flight, . . . He spoke to the *tzaddikim* of the past and was taught directly by Elijah the Prophet. He knew the future and all that was occurring and why. All of this he achieved without the use of practical Kabbalah.

2. Introduction to *Sefer HaChinuch*. The six cities of refuge were established in ancient Israel for the protection of those who committed unintentional manslaughter [Num. 35:25-34]. The "manslaughter" alluded to in our context is spiritual self-destruction. See further, n. 29 below.

3. All *mitzvot* act on reality; the six *mitzvot* being discussed, however, are states of consciousness. Chassidism explains that these states have to be experienced to such a degree that they have a physical effect on the heart or brain (e.g., that they cause a change in the brain cells). This implies that the meditation requires ever-increasing intensity. In this respect, Rabbi Saadia Gaon taught that one has to make *tshuvah* (repent) for one's previous consciousness of God (i.e., the way one performed the six commandments)—even that of a moment before.

The Torah contains 613 *mitzvot* which can be categorized in various ways: positive (affirmative action) and negative (prohibitions); on whom they devolve (e.g., the king, priests, the whole people); when they apply (e.g., when the Temple is standing, etc.); and so forth. See further, Ch. III, sect. 3: True Actions: *Mitzvot*.

4. Simple faith is beyond the dualities of the mind. This is expressed in a well-known *gematria* in relation to Purim: the phrase "Bless Mordechai" (good) equals in *gematria* the phrase "curse Haman" (evil). Each of the phrases equals in *gematria* "simple faith"—indicating the state of consciousness above mind where apparent good and evil are in truth one (analogous to + and − electrical charges)—the state of consciousness to be achieved on Purim. (See further, Ch. II, n. 16 on *Gematria*, and n. 9, on *Keter*.)

5. *Netzah* is eternity or immortality; the conquest of time and death, leading to absolute security and trust in the Infinite (its inner attribute). In *Netzach* exist the motivating drives which seek to conquer all that would interfere or restrict its ambition, that is, to conquer all states of confinement.

6. Modern slavery is primarily enslavement to future economic security, living for the future at the expense of the present. In this respect, the numerous Jewish holidays and especially the *Shabbat*, on which work is prohibited, all "commemorate the Exodus from Egypt".

7. The Sages say that the Torah was only given to those who ate manna in Sinai. Manna (*man* in Hebrew) is related to the same Hebrew root as faith (*emunah*). Trust in living in the present is symbolized by the manna which fell each day from heaven but could not be stored. For *Shabbat*, two portions of manna fell on Friday. When a person tasted manna, he tasted whatever food he imagined.

8. This commandment is particularly associated with the Jewish mission: "Whoever renounces idolatry is called Jew" [*R. Yochanan, Megillah* 13a].

9. There are two kinds of intermediaries. One cuts the relationship between a person and the Infinite, and substitutes itself for God. The other serves as a channel or power center which assists the direct connection with God, as in the case of *tzaddikim*.

10. *Yerushalmi Kiddushin* 4:12; *Ta'anit* 22b. See Zimmerman, Ibid., pp. 124-125.

11. Enjoying without blessing, however, is called stealing, *Yerushalmi Nedarim* 9:1; *Berachot* 35b.

12. The *Shema* mentions two names of God: the Tetragrammaton (*Adonai*), which signifies God's attribute of mercy (*Tiferet*); and Elokim, which signifies His attribute of judgment (*Gevurah*). The inner meaning of Judge is the "provider of life"; the judgment being in terms of how much life energy is given.

13. It is stated in *Tikuney Zohar* 66 (98a), that ". . . when a man comes together with his wife, he must remove all clothing to be together with her as one. . . . Likewise, one must remove all other 'garments' when he makes unification twice each day, declaring, '*Shema Israel . . .*' "

14. A simple but fundamental *gematria* is that the word "one" (13) equals the word "love" (13); "one" plus "love" equals the Tetragrammaton (26). See on *Gematria*, Ch. II, n. 16.

15. *Sotah* 47a.

16. See *Tanya*, Ch. 40.

17. Also called the "animal" or primitive brain. The higher the species, the

more it includes or carries within itself all previous forms of life. This is the analogue on the physical level of the inner-inclusion of the spiritual Worlds, one within the other within the psyche. The microcosm of man includes all previous incarnations within both his body and his psyche. See Overview, sect. 2: The Five Worlds; and Ch. V, sect. 2: Reincarnation.

18. *Zohar*, Vol. I, 153b. This is an explanation of the tendency of kabbalists to be extremely careful to protect the purity of their imagination, and thus to be very strict with respect to modesty and to all matters of relation to the other sex.

19. The term *kabbalah* is derived from the Hebrew root meaning both "received" and "parallel": received parallels.

Da'at (Knowledge) is the attachment of mind to the idea. *Da'at* exists when the person develops a deep concern and identification with the concept developed by *Binah*. It is the power to make decisions that results from the abstract thought of *Chochmah-Binah*. *Da'at* is the synthesis of the triad between *Chochmah* and *Binah*, and as well, draws the power of thought into the emotions. In this context, *Da'at* is called the "soul" of the *Midot*.

20. *Bereshit Rabbah* 3:9. See also *Shabbat* 55a referring to the shattering of *Tohu*.

21. See Overview, sect. 4: The Breaking of the Vessels; and sect. 6: Rectification of Reality.

22. In the early Freudian circle, the development of psychoanalysis was considered to be of messianic importance. The roots of psychoanalysis in the Jewish understanding of and approach to the psyche are becoming more known. George Steiner, for example, notes the influence "of Talmudic exegesis from which so much of the spirit of Freud's hermeneutics was derived." Steiner, *Real Presences* (U. Chicago Press, 1989), pp. 46-47. See in particular, D. Bakan, *Sigmund Freud and the Jewish Mystical Tradition* (Princeton, 1958). Much research remains to be done in this area.

Prior familiarity with Freud's basic approach in part accounts for the more ready acceptance of his ideas in Jewish circles. For example, the earliest public presentation of the theory of dream interpretation was made to the Vienna B'nai B'rit where it received an "enthusiastic reception". See also, D. Klein, *Jewish Origins of the Psychoanalytic Movement* (U. Chicago Press, 1981).

In respect to repression, it is told of certain Chassidic Rebbes in the *Chabad* tradition that when they found themselves shocked by a confession of one of their Chassidim, they would retire and meditate until they brought to consciousness that variant of evil in themselves. Being shocked (a sign of the unconscious), they feared they had repressed the evil (*helem ha'ra*).

23. *Magid Devarav LeYaakov* (Jerusalem, 1971), 52; as translated by A. Kaplan, *Meditation and Kabbalah* (Weiser, 1982), p. 286; p. 290, see also Keter *Keter Shem Tov* 207.

24. The total space of consciousness can be related to the concept of building the temple (or a "spiritual chariot") around the self. A person's awareness of his relation to God is his continuous state of prayer in the temple.

The symbol in the Torah for complete clarity of consciousness is the Tablets of the Ten Commandments which were cubes measuring six handbreadths in each direction [*Batra* 14a]. The engraved letters of the Tablets could be read the same from all sides [Exodus 32:15].

The cube, which has twenty-seven elements (eight points, twelve lines, six surfaces, one volume) equals in *gematria zach*, "pure"; in turn, "pure" is the root of the word "glass" (*zechuchit*).

25. Thus it is taught "there is no left in the Ancient One (the level of *Keter*), for all is right". This means that, at the superconscious level, awe or fear of God (left) is indistinguishable from the highest manifestation of love (right).

26. The seven *mitzvot* form the basis for a Jewish meditation which is drawn solely from its own tradition. The meditator may visualize himself as inside the cube or "temple" defined by the six directions, each of which faces infinity. The meditation is the progressive breaking through barriers or shells met in respect to each of the six aspects of consciousness—as one's total universe is expanding.

A person may notice a tendency to dwell on one or two dimensions because they are particularly relevant to his immediate situation. The emphasis, however, is upon the *whole* of consciousness, not solely upon its aspects. The process of clarification involves the realization, at progressively deeper levels, of the interdependence and indivisible unity of all aspects of consciousness. As the meditation progresses, one is brought closer and closer to the infinite present. See also n. 3 above.

27. The cube of each dimension "gives birth" to the next higher dimension. Thus a three dimensional cube has twenty-seven (3^3) elements; a four dimensional hypercube has eighty-one (3^4) elements, etc.

The hypercube is the geometric form often used to represent the idea of fourth dimensionality. The hypercube has sixteen faces and eight hyperfaces (shared faces) alluding to the concept of inter-penetration or inter-inclusion of levels of consciousness as described by Kabbalah. See further, Kaplan, *The Bahir*; Ibid., pp. 104-107. For more on the properties of the hypercube, see A. Dewdney, *A Program for Rotating Hypercubes Induces Fourth Dimensional Dementia*; Scientific American, April, 1986; and more generally on the fourth dimension, R. v. B. Rucker, *Geometry, Relativity and the Fourth Dimension* (Dover, 1977).

28. Five dimensional space has ten infinity points or co-ordinates which relate to the *sefirot*. Each of the *sefirot* is a potential dimension when lived fully in its own right; for example, if one lived out all of the aspects of love represented by the ten sub-*sefirot* of *Chesed*. An attempt to realize what this can mean may form the basis for further exploratory meditation; in other words, if one were to apply the cube structure to each of the six *mitzvot* separately.

29. The Torah promises that,

> . . . the Lord your God will expand your boundaries as He has sworn to your forefathers, provided you keep all of these commandments; to love the Lord and to always walk in his ways, you shall then add for yourselves three more cities. [Deut. 19:8-9]

Thus it is interpreted that in the future, three additional *mitzvot* ("cities of refuge") will become continuous—expressing the full potentiality of consciousness as expressed by the ten dimensions of the *sefirot*.

30. "You cannot see My face; for no man shall see Me and live" [Exod. 33:19-20].

31. Maimonides, *Mishnah Torah, Sanhedrin*, Ch. 10.

Chapter VII

Union

The innate desire of the soul is to reunify with the infinite. This is the root of every wanting; no other object, idea, or love can satisfy its desire. It is not only what the soul wants but what all of existence wants.[1] In the moment of union a person experiences all of existence uniting in himself— and all of its suffering, all of its yearning.[2] This moment, as well as lower levels of mystical experience, is usually referred to as *devekut*[3] (being bound to, clinging, or cleaving to God) but also as "prophecy" and *ahdut* (becoming united, unification). The experience of *devekut*, however, is seldom elaborated upon in pre-Chassidic Kabbalah.[4] The famous Talmudic story of the "four Sages who entered Paradise" expresses the dangers involved in the highest levels of transcendent experience.[5] We read that Ben Azzai died, Ben Zoma became insane, Elisha Ben Abuyah renounced his faith, and only Rabbi Akiva "entered in [the state of] *shalom* and went out in *shalom*". In Chassidism, it is taught that while the other Sages did not commit themselves to return before the onset of their ascent towards God, Rabbi Akiva did. So that upon achieving union he naturally (unconsciously) returned. This is interpreted to reflect his commitment to the rectification of reality, which is the enduring value and purpose of union.[6]

As the story of the four Talmudic Sages illustrates, mystical experience is inherently unstable, and is as potentially dangerous to the psyche as is its power of illumination. The process of "running towards God" is inevitably followed by a fall into ordinary consciousness. Falling is part of the natural spiritual rhythm in which transcendent experience is integrated into the routine of daily life. In order to achieve this integration, it is best that a person be committed to the spiritual path with its structure and collective experience, and if possible, to a teacher. If not, he may draw conclusions in isolation which lead into extreme asceticism, or egoism (most commonly in the form of messianism), or into psychosis. The ambivalent attitude of the Sages towards mystical experience is reflected in the teaching:

Better is one hour of *tshuvah* and good actions in this world than the whole of life in the world to come; and better is one hour of the bliss of the spirit in the world to come than all the life in this world. [Sayings of the Fathers, 4:17]

For such reasons the writings of Kabbalah are coded; its language and imagery is designed both to reveal and to conceal. Nevertheless, mystical union is the hidden core of Kabbalah,[7] and is at the root of its total understanding.[8]

1. Meditation

The traditional practices used by kabbalists to achieve *devekut* often involved Hebrew letter combinations and the recitation and permutation of divine names. These techniques are principally associated with the 13th century kabbalist Rabbi Abraham Abulafia and his school which in turn drew upon ancient sources.[9] Letter combination and meditation on the names of God are still used by kabbalists and their students today (Figure 4). The intention of these meditations is explained by the Italian kabbalist Rabbi Moshe Chaim Luzzatto:[10]

God decreed . . . that when one would utter His Name, divine illumination and influence would be bestowed upon him. This is what God means when he says [Exodus 20:21], 'In every place where I allow My name to be mentioned, I will come to you and bless you.'

When a particular name of God is uttered and used to call upon Him, it will result in the emanation of an influence (*hashpa'ah*) associated with that Name . . . God decreed that inspiration and prophecy should be attained in this manner. . . . This occurs when one repeats one of these Names mentally, utters it verbally, or combines it with other words, and at the same time fulfills all the other conditions. . . .

Prayer, singing, meditation, secluded and silent communion with God, and speaking directly to God are the main paths to *devekut*. In prayer, the kabbalist concentrates his mind on the inner mystical intentions (*kavvanot*) and specific rectifications associated with each word or phrase (Figure 4). In meditation (*hitbonenut*),[11] which may involve concentration upon spiritual ideas for many hours,[12] the meditator reaches out through the intellect and then beyond. Such contemplation, although in a less concentrated form, is the essence of Torah study. The happiness which accompanies contemplation of the Torah (associated with *Binah*), underlies the great

Figure 4 **Rabbi Shalom Sharabi's Mystical Intentions on the first word of the Amidah Prayer:** *Baruch* (Bless)

Jewish emphasis upon learning. The phenomenon of Jewish study for its own sake, of men spending the greatest part of their lives "learning", is that of lifelong meditation. Nevertheless, no matter how much is gained in this way, it is not considered comparable to knowledge gained through direct spiritual inspiration.[13]

"Turning one's face to God" is the direct and most uniquely Jewish approach to union.[14] As is described by Rabbi Moshe Chaim Luzzatto, one is—

> ... imploring and entreating Him and being heard and listened to by the Blessed One in the same way that a man, speaking to his friend, is heard and listened to by him.[15]

Direct communion usually develops in the mind before being overtly spoken. One's inner conversation is the continuation of Abraham's and Sarah's conversation. In the Jewish tradition, this right can be considered the inheritance and entitlement from the ancestors (*z'chut avot*); an inheritance which includes the right to argue with God and to question his providence and justice.[16] When communion involves actual speaking or spontaneous speech, it may be called *sichah*. *Sichah* (conversation) is simply intimate speaking out loud to God. (The daily practice of *sichah*, which is strongly emphasized by Rabbi Nachman, is nevertheless called *hitbodedut* in his writings.) In general, Jewish prayer or communion begins with praise. But each person begins at his own beginning; one with silence, another with singing, another by speaking of the difficulty of speaking, etc.[17] This opening is called "the arousal from below", the creation of an opening in oneself in which the infinite may "dwell". Eventually, perhaps after many periods of silence and deadness, a person's speaking will be answered by the experience of the divine presence.

2. Song Meditation

Song always implies pleasure; even a song of pain is a song longing for life's pleasure. Each and every part of the Creation sings to its Creator.[18] In terms of the *sefirot*, both the root of song and of primordial pleasure are in the second head of *Keter*, the Head of Nothingness (*Resha d'ayin*), which is also the root of primordial pleasure. The Head of Nothingness is also the root of the Torah; thus Torah itself is called song, and is sung out. Singing is pure speech; the union of air, water, and fire.[19] Thus *chassidim* often begin the study of Torah with the singing of several *niggunim* (wordless songs) which open the learning with their rhythms and transcendent structures.

Song meditation is known from the time of the prophets and their schools. Music is both an analogy for the movement towards mystical experience, and also an actual technique used to achieve *devekut*.[20] In meditation, the singer sings with God's presence before his eyes:[21]

> Sing, *tzadikkim*, to the Name . . . so that this name is before you, in order that you unify in such a way that the song is the complete *devekut*. . . .

Singing is the dark path, the blind search of the lover.[22] When a person enters into singing, he is searching for the Beloved One.[23] Thus the Song of Songs (called the Holy of the Holies of the Torah)[24] is the allegory of the love between the bride and groom, between the soul and God.

Poetry and song are the same word in Hebrew, *shir*. The song is intense being that disappears, whereas the poem is engraved or perhaps coarsens into words. The song that is sung expresses the upward motion, the stripping away of words. Poetry is the downward motion of enclothement, of capturing. Thus poetry is related to the concept in Torah of catching light, of catching arrows in midair; ultimately, of catching the expanding universe. Poetry is a power to catch something that is about to disappear. This power of the soul to catch comes from the Higher Mother, *Binah*. The power to catch the arrow is greater than the shooting itself. The poet hears singing and somehow tries to catch it. The poem expresses the outer limit and beyond what he has words for. His desire to preserve and to express it must be stronger than the experience itself. Form must be stronger than inspiration. The female must be stronger than the male. If experience is stronger, if there are no words, it disappears into being.

3. Mystical Union

Chashmal is associated with the light experienced in mystical union. (In modern Hebrew, it means "electricity"). It is mentioned three times in Ezekiel's visions of the Chariot:[25]

> . . . Upon the likeness of the throne was the likeness of the appearance of a man above upon it. And I saw something like the eye of *chashmal* [out of the midst of the fire]; . . . and there was a brightness about him. . . . [Ezek. 1:26.]

In this context, Rabbi Dov Baer of Mezritch said that when a man ascends all the worlds and becomes one with God, he is called Adam, ". . . being transformed into the cosmic figure of the primordial man whose likeness is upon the throne that Ezekiel beheld". By this is meant that only when a person achieves union does he become the complete man, Adam.[26] In the moment of union, God dissolves the physical and psychic image of man that His light has created. At that moment, every thought, every need resolves; there is no desire to go on, there is nowhere else. Mystical union is therefore the only actual experience of the truth.

The experience of union is beyond adequate verbal description, and is relative to each person's unique experience. Nevertheless, within these limitations, an attempt will be made to indicate the experience as involving several levels or movements. The approach towards union may be felt as deepening and more compelling waves or pulses opening out of each other. The first impulse can be said to involve an inner movement of return, of arousal from below. This is the initial state of self-negation, of "lowliness" (*shiflut*; associated with *Malchut*), of the self experiencing itself for what it really is—of having no power of its own, of deserving nothing. A yielding of oneself into all that it means to be human, into life itself.

As a person becomes aware of the divine dimension, he fears the approaching precipice. Yielding, giving his life up completely—everything of time, of place, of form is suddenly subsumed in inconceivable brightness. Blinded, he sees blindly, seeing from all parts of his being at once. Seeing the image of reality emerging from light, birth and death from light, good and evil from light, the formation of objects from light. He knows with absolute certainty that this infinite, incomprehensible light is God's love, that God's love is the only reality.

In the "embrace" of light (phosphorous light; white, non-human light) he knows happiness from the very beginning of his existence, from the beginning of all existence. Happiness so deep that there is nothing left. Here is where he comes from, where freedom comes from. Chassidism explains that the white light of *chashmal* is an expression of God's joy (*simchah*) that union is taking place, and a protection or garment enclothing the union. This light or brilliant happiness may be associated with the light which emanates from *Binah*, the Higher Mother—the level of the higher return.[27]

Within the unbearable intensity, a light of even greater being opens. With this inner light comes the direct awareness of the absolute meaning of existence, that man's life—his own life—is ultimately and eternally meaningful. The experiencing of purpose is the deepest point, the most personal and enduring point, his most fundamental consolation: that the suffering and hopelessness is worthwhile, that he trusts God—trusts what He is doing by making him live.

As he is turned away, the top of his mind in the afterglow or the impression of the light of *chashmal*, he falls back in the continuous, cyclic process of *tshuvah*. But he remains in expectation, the "silent, thin voice" within inviting in silence, in a state of inner hovering to return.

Prayer, meditation, and deep song are occasions for the continuous striving for union, occasions when the impression of a previous union may be revitalized so that the glow of *chashmal* is constantly in the mind, and that the seed continues to be fertile. Now more emphatically, however, he is seeking to achieve his lifework.[28] The experience of purpose is the deepest experience of Jewish mysticism. It is the mystical foundation of its affirmation of this world, and of the commitment to its rectification. Something presses to be born into the world; otherwise the union has been a sterile ecstasy. Action completes union.[29]

Chashmal is also regarded by the Sages as a category of angels called *chashmalim* ("living angels of fire speaking").[30] The function of the *chashmalim* is to test souls about to enter into the secrets of the Torah. They do this by "talking" more and more rapidly. To the extent that one can understand the angels, one receives permission to enter. They speak faster and faster, and souls drop out at different levels of experience. Rapport means that a person can "talk back". This applies not only to mystical experience but to communion with all aspects of the Creation. The sky talks fast, asking one to reply. If one talks back just as fast, one can get into the sky. It is as though each reality had a guard standing outside it. The key to getting in is to be in its oscillation, in the same vibration. Every created thing has a "mouth", everything in the world is "talking" very fast, inviting you.[31]

The *chashmalim* can be related to the flame of the revolving sword held by the angels guarding the entrance to the Garden [Gen. 3:24], called "the metamorphosing blade". The revolving blade hints at the "fast talk" of the angels, the barrier of oscillation. The ability to understand for a moment or longer the talk of the *chashmalim* of the physical world is analogous to the ability to enter into the experience of union from ordinary consciousness. The *chashmalim* (the outer light of *chashmal*) "guard" the entrance to the union. Once within the union, the inner *chashmal* expresses the "silent-speaking" of purpose experienced within the surrounding light. To the extent that a person is able to remain conscious in the experience of union, the deeper he may penetrate into the inner reality of his own and of all existence, and the more of all that he has experienced in his life is lifted with him. The greatest mystic is nevertheless an imperfect man; a man of a particular soul who brings with him limited although new experience. The knowledge of Kabbalah is the collective experience of the generations since Abraham first knew the one God; it is the expression of Jewish consciousness itself in union with the light of Infinity.

NOTES

1. Rabbi Shneor Zalman, author of the central work of *Chabad Chassidism*, writes in *Tanya*:

> [Like a flame which seeks to be parted from the wick] so does the *neshama* (soul) of man . . . naturally desire and yearn to separate itself . . . from the body . . . though thereby it would . . . completely lose its identity, with nothing remaining of its former essence and being. . . .

Tanya, Ch. 19 (Kehot, 1973). Nevertheless, it is taught that the soul maintains its uniqueness for eternity.

2. Rabbi Nachman writes:

> . . . [I]n as much as Israel performing the will of . . . and are integrated . . . in the unity of God . . . thereby the entire world is integrated . . . However, one does not merit it save by the complete self-annihilation (*bitul*) . . . until one becomes integrated in His unity. . . .
>
> He annihilates himself and does not care for himself at all; he feels the anguish of Israel, his friend, and by the annihilation he is integrated in the *ayin*.

Likkutei Moharan, Vol. I, 50; and: Vol. I, 22:10.

3. Thus Rabbi Shneor Zalman in *Commentary on the Siddur*, p. 51:

> This is the true cleaving (*devekut*), as he becomes one substance with God in whom he is swallowed, without being separate so as to be a distinct entity at all.

See further Professor Idel's article, "Universalization and Integration: Two Conceptions of Mystical Union in Jewish Mysticism", in Idel and McGinn (eds.), *Mystical Union and Monotheistic Faith: An Ecumenical Dialogue* (Macmillan, 1989), in particular pp. 44-46 where he discusses the above quotations.

On the entire subject of mystical experience in Judaism, see the pioneering work of Professor Moshe Idel in the works cited throughout this Chapter. See also two works by L. Jacobs, *On Ecstacy* (Rossel Books, 1963), a translation of the book by Rabbi Dov Baer of *Lubavitch*, the son of the founder of *Chabad Chassidism*, and *Jewish Mystical Testimonies* (Schocken, 1976).

4. This is so for several important reasons. Most basically, the goal of Judaism is not the achievement of individual mystical experience but rather the rectification of ordinary life. As such, the importance of *devekut* is to increase the commitment

and power of one's performance of *mitzvot*. The proper performance of the *mitzvot*, therefore, is a central focus of kabbalistic meditation and practice.

It should be noted in this respect that the distinct word or concept of "mysticism", and also of "religion", is foreign to Judaism. (In Hebrew, the word used for "religion" is *dat*, which simply means "law" or "regulated practice"; "mysticism" is a borrowed word in modern Hebrew.) Either concept, religion or mysticism, separates the relation with God from the full life in this world. Thus Judaism emphasizes the performance of *mitzvot* which binds ordinary reality with the higher or inner reality, a binding which is re-established day after day.

Another reason for reticence is that mystical experience is considered to be a gift from God, possibly as a reward (the highest reward in this world) for merit achieved in past reincarnations. The fact that a person has been granted this gift does not confirm his perfection as a human being. As God says in this regard: "I will be gracious (*chen*; grace) to whom I will be gracious" [Exod. 33:19].

Further caution is reflected in certain rabbinic opinions which required that a person be 40 years old and married, or have mastered the oral and written law before studying Kabbalah. It should be mentioned that these opinions were not strictly followed in the past nor are they today. This is especially so now because of the availability of reliable commentaries which explain the intricacies and potentially misleading aspects of Kabbalah. These requirements were never applied to the study of Chassidism which deals with the direct sexual imagery of Kabbalah in psychological terms.

A valuable discussion may be found in Steinsaltz, *The Strife of the Spirit*; Ibid., Ch. 22: "Religion and Mystical Powers".

5. *Chigigah* 14a. The ultimate culmination of the experience of union is known as "dying in the kiss" [Deut. 34:5]. This is the death of Moses, of certain mystics, and of many martyrs. Below is an early kabbalistic description of the ascent of Ben Azzai, one of the four discussed above, who was not turned back:

> "Ben Azzai looked and died." He gazed at the radiance of the *Shekhinah*, like a man with weak eyes who gazes into the full light of the sun . . . Thus it happened to Ben Azzai: the light overwhelmed him, and he gazed at it because of his great desire to cleave to it . . . , and after he cleaved to it he did not wish to be separated from the sweet radiance, and he remained immersed and hidden in it. And, as it is said: "for no man shall see Me and live" . . . But Ben Azzai only gazed at it a little while, and his soul departed and remained . . . [in the] most precious light.

Translated by Idel, *New Perspectives*, Ibid., pp. 35-36.

6. *Tanya*, Ch. 36. It is likewise taught that Nadav and Avihu, the two elder sons of Aaron who were burned up upon offering incense in a non-prescribed fashion on the inauguration day of the Tabernacle [Lev. 10:1], were also guilty of "running" without prior commitment to return.

7. As Rabbi Nachman explains:

When a person merits to be integrated in the [Light of] *Ain Sof*, his Torah and prayer are those of God Himself. . . . Since he is integrated in the One and is one with God, he lives eternally just as God does. And there is no perfection but the perfection of God. . . . Where a man's mind is, there is the whole man. He who knows, and attains to a divine understanding, is really there. The greater his knowing, the more he is integrated . . . in God.

Likkutei Moharan, I, 22, par. 10; and I, 21, par. 11.

8. Thus the chassidic Rebbe, R. Menahem Mendel:

[T]he concealed matters in the *Zohar* and the writing of the *Ari* are those based upon the cleaving (*devekut*) to God, [and] for those who are worthy to cleave and to see the supernal Chariot [of Ezekiel's vision] . . . the paths of the firmament are clear and he walks on them [seeing his way] with his mental eyes. . . .

Quoted in Idel, *Kabbalah, New Perspectives* (Yale U. Press, 1988), p. 58.

9. On Abulafia, see the two recent books by Professor Idel of the Hebrew University: *The Mystical Experience in Abraham Abulafia* (SUNY Press, 1988); and *Studies in Ecstatic Kabbalah* (SUNY Press, 1988).

On Jewish meditation in general, see A. Kaplan, *Meditation and the Bible* (Weiser, 1978); *Meditation and the Kabbalah* (Weiser, 1982); and *Jewish Meditation: A Practical Guide* (Schocken, 1985).

10. Luzzatto, *The Way of God* (Feldheim, 1981), Ch. 2. Generally, however, the use of such techniques is restricted because of the danger that the adept may be insufficiently prepared, or that they will be misused or idolized.

11. These terms are not used in a consistent way throughout the writings of Judaism. See for example the treatment of *hitbodedut* by A. Kaplan, *Meditation and the Bible*; Ibid., Ch. 7, and by Prof. Idel, *Studies in Ecstatic Kabbalah*, Ibid. Ch. 7.

12. The Talmud reports that "the early *hasidim* (pious ones) used to wait one hour before praying (and one hour afterwards) in order to concentrate their minds." [*Ber.* 30b]. Nine hours (three hours three times a day) were devoted to meditative prayer. A hint as to the nature of their meditation (perhaps involving the transcendent light of *Ain Sof*) is alluded to by Rabbi Eliezer Azikri, a 16th century kabbalist in Safed—

. . . they would imagine the light of the *Shekhinah* (God's presence) above their heads as though it were flowing all around them and they were sitting in the midst of light.

Kaplan, Ibid., p. 84; and Idel, *Kabbalah, New Perspectives*; Ibid., pp. 99-100.

One of the postures known in Jewish meditation is that of the head down between the knees, representing in-turning, or even the return to the womb. This posture is also associated with the concept of the "end enwedged into the beginning". This is called the "brain power of mother". The female posture represents the internalization of reality; the search for the infinite through the self, through subjectivity. This posture expresses the finite seeking the infinite. The opposite posture (associated with Reb Isaac of Homil), with the head arched completely back, is called the "brain power of the father". This position (also a singing posture) represents openness; the expressing of the infinite through the negation of self.

13. M. Luzzatto, *The Way of God*; Ibid., p. 173.

14. This practice is described by Rabbi Azikri—

... At the appropriate times one should withdraw to a secluded place [*hitbodedut*] ... [and] lift one's eyes ... to the one King, the Cause of all causes ... ; as in water face answereth to face [Prov. 37:19]. ... As man turns his face to God so also will He turn to him, and they will cleave together [in mystical communion].

See R. J. Zwi Werblowsky, *Joseph Karo, Lawyer and Mystic* (JPS, 1980), pp. 63-66.

15. M. Luzzatto, *The Path of the Just* (Feldheim, 1966), p. 231.

16. For example, Abraham's arguing with God over the fate of Sodom [Gen. 18:19-33]. Occasionally God reveals his approval of those who contend with him directly (as in the case of Job) while rejecting the well-meaning defenders of His justice [Job 32:7].

17. A related form of meditation (associated with the Kotz *chassidim*) is designed to achieve truth in speech. The goal is to reach a point where one is able to say exactly what one means. One literally plucks voices, cliches, and foreign phrases out of one's mouth (and mind), as well as the exaggerating or polemical elements which creep into expression. It is like weeding one's mouth, a process which becomes more and more subtle as one progresses. This meditation can be arduous and extend over a period of time (a day or a week), and of course is never-ending. The result is a coming back to the stark truth and the silence of oneself. In *sichah*, however, one becomes aware of every inner lie, even if unconscious, because it is impossible to speak to God falsely.

18. *Midrash Perek Shirah.*

19. The throat is the top of the heart, the heart ascending. The deeper the song in the throat, the more the voice is burning. The top of the mouth (the palate) is the bottom of the brain. Water (*Chochmah*) flows down from the mind into the song, and fire (*Binah*) ascends from the heart. Breath (*Da'at*) is the power to unify water and fire. The shape of the voice is the shape of fire.

20. It is reported that the chassidic Rebbe Mical of Zlotchov, known as possessing "the key to the Chamber of Music", requested that he never be left alone by his *chassidim* because he feared the intensity of his singing. Nevertheless, because of an oversight, he was left alone in his room and not restrained, and it is reported that he died in the kiss while singing a certain *niggun*. According to one tradition, this *niggun* has been preserved by the Breslov *chassidim*. See Ben Zion Solomon, "*Asader Lisudoso*," a songbook of traditional music of the Breslov *chassidim*. A tape of these *niggunim* is available from Breslov Research Institute, P.O. Box 5370, Jerusalem, Israel.

21. As brought by the kabbalist R. Elijah de Vidas; Idel, *Kabbalah, New Perspectives*; Ibid., p. 51. See also, Idel, *The Mystical Experience in A. Abulafia*, Ch. 2: "Music and Ecstatic Kabbalah" (SUNY, 1988).

22. . . . One should arise after midnight and give praise to Him, practice solitude and enjoy His love . . . , calling God fond names, singing to the Beloved: it is the custom of passionate lovers to sing, and since the love of our Creator is wonderful, passing the love of women, therefore he who loves Him with all his heart should sing before Him.

Rabbi Eliezer Azikri, *Sefer Hasidim* (written c. 1583). Werblowsky, Ibid., pp. 57-58. The arising at midnight for the prayer-meditation *tikkun hatzoth* (midnight rectification) is still practiced.

23. Eve is called "the mother of all life" [Gen. 3:20], which is also understood as, the mother of "being alive," that is, of all transcendent experience.

In kabbalistic terms, the Song of Songs is the unification of *Malchut* with *Tiferet*, which is the same mystical intention (*kavannah*) which kabbalists and many others utter (or think) before performing a *mitzvah*.

24. *Yadayim* 3:5 in the name of Rabbi Akiva.

25. And I looked, and behold, a storm wind came out of the north, a great cloud, and fire flaring up, as it were the colour of [*chashmal*], out of the midst of the fire. . . .

Rashi says it is forbidden to interpret the verse which includes reference to *chashmal* in Ezekiel's vision of the Chariot (*Merkavah*); in Kabbalah, however, it is interpreted.

Literally, *chash* is silence and *mal* is speech, which can be interpreted as referring to the silent-speaking surrounding and within the experience of union.

26. Quoted in G. Scholem, *The Messianic Idea in Judaism* (Schocken, 1971), pp. 226-227. "*Chashmal*" is equal in *gematria* to "garment". See *Etz Chaim* 26:2, 41:1.

27. See further, Ch. IV, sect. 2: Returning Home.

28. This experience can also be considered the basis of the famous story of Rebbe Zusha of Annipol, the chassidic mystic who said that in the World to Come he will not be asked why he was not as great as Moses, but why he was not Zusha, and the basis of the *Baal Shem Tov*'s teaching that every Jew is an only son of God.

29. The following is a quotation from Rabbi Abraham Abulafia which, upon careful study, reveals many of the techniques as well as the progression of experience discussed above:

Be prepared for your God, oh Israelite! Make yourself ready to direct your heart to God alone. Cleanse the body and choose a lonely house where none shall hear your voice. . . . If thou can, do it . . . during the night. In the hour when you prepare yourself to speak with the Creator and you wish Him to reveal His might to you, then be careful to abstract all your thought from the vanities of this world. Cover yourself with your prayer shawl and put *tefillin* on your head and hands that you may be filled with awe of the *Shekhinah* which is near you.

Cleanse your clothes, and, if possible, let all your garments be white, for all this is helpful in leading the heart towards the fear of God and the love of God. If it is night, kindle many lights, until all is bright. Then take ink, pen and table to your hand and remember that you are about to serve God in joy. ˙. . . Now begin to pen a few or many letters, to permute and to combine them until your heart is warm. Then be mindful of their movements and of what you can bring forth by moving them. And when you feel that your heart is already warm and when you see that by combinations of letters you can grasp new things which by human tradition or by yourself you would not be able to know and when you are thus prepared to receive the flux of divine power which flows into you, then turn all your true thought to imagine the Name and His exalted angels in your heart as if they were human beings sitting or standing about you. . . .

Having imagined this very vividly, turn your whole mind to understand with your thoughts the many things which will come into your heart through the letters imagined. Ponder them . . . like one to whom a parable or a dream is being related, and as one who meditates on a deep problem in a scientific book. . . . And all this will happen to you after having flung away tablet and quill or after they will have dropped from you because of the intensity of your thought.

And know, the stronger the intellectual flux within you, the weaker will become your outer and your inner parts. Your whole body will be seized by an extremely strong trembling, so that you will think that surely you are about to die, because your soul, overjoyed with its knowledge, will leave your body. And be ready at this moment consciously to choose death, and then you shall know that you have come far enough to receive the influx.

And then wishing to honor the glorious Name by serving it with the life of body and soul, veil your face and be afraid to look at God. Then return to the matters of the body, rise and eat and drink a little, or refresh yourself with a pleasant odor, and restore your spirit to its sheath until another time, and rejoice at your lot and know that God loves you!

Quoted in Sholem, *Major Trends in Jewish Mysticism* (Shocken, 1941), pp. 136-137.
   30. *Chagigah* 13b.
   31. When Moses hit the rock when he was commanded to speak to it, he broke with God's will, and therefore with nature as well [Num. 20:7-12]. By talking to the rock, it would then have freely released its water (*Chochmah*). Instead he forced the rock, thus imposing his will over God's will. This is related to the fall of Adam, through which man lost his primary connection with nature. Adam's power to give animals their names symbolized his ability to talk to each species, to resonate in rhythm with each of their natures. Moses' punishment was analogous to that of Adam's, that of being forbidden entry to the land of Israel which is the potential Garden in existence.

Chapter VIII

Pleasing the Land of Israel

1. A Microcosm of Reality

The land of Israel is the center of the Jewish universe. "This is Jerusalem. I have set her in the midst of the nations, and countries are round about her" [Ezek. 5:5]. In the Cave of Machpelah in Hebron are buried the Patriarchs and Matriarchs who express the land's character, just as they are the archetypes of the Jewish pysche. According to the *Midrash*, at the center of Israel is Jerusalem. The center of Jerusalem is the Temple, and its center is the Holy of Holies. Under the Holy of Holies is the Foundation Stone, the point from which the world evolves. And just as Jerusalem is the center of its physical world, it is the epicenter of Jewish consciousness.

Three continents meet along the narrow landmass of Israel: the scrub landscape of Mediterranean Europe, the Arabian deserts and the steppes of Central Asia, and the Rift Valley of Africa. Within its borders are the snow-peaked mountains of the Hermon, the marshlands of the Hula Valley, the sub-tropical Lake Kinneret, the desolation of the Dead Sea, the Negev and Sinai deserts, the coral reefs of the Red Sea, the palms and sand dunes of the south coast, the open wheat plains of the northern Negev, the beaches of the Mediterranean Sea, the fertile coastal plains of citrus orchards, the high ridges of Jerusalem and its steppes, and the pine-wooded hills and steep wadis of the upper Galilee—a multitude of habitats for an extraordinary range of plants, birds, and animals.[1]

Although the land of Israel was promised to Abraham and his seed, it is God's land given as a conditional gift: "[F]or the land is Mine, and you are strangers and sojourners with Me" [Lev. 25:23]. It is not ordinary land but rather the partner created as a "help-mate against" (*ezer k'negdo*) the Jewish people; a land which "wills to do the will of the Creator".[2] Laws such as those regarding the Sabbatical Year, agriculture, and *Shabbat* guarantee its fertility and independence of being. This gift of the land must be continually deserved. The condition is that Israel be a holy people, that the people live up to the potential of the idea of Israel. In other words, the land

84

is given to the Jewish people in order to achieve the eternal purpose. As commitment to this purpose fades, possession becomes less and less secure. The land of Israel is the testing ground, the truth ground for the Jewish people. God's eyes are always upon it, "from the beginning of the year even unto the end of the year" [Deut. 11, 12].

Here live Jews from almost every country on earth, speaking every major language: Ashkenazim from Europe, Sephardim from Arab lands, Ethiopians from Africa, Yemenites, Indians, Australians, North Americans and South Americans. Jews who are divided ethnically, politically, economically, religiously, and yet are one body, one heart, and one nervous system. All the tribes are gathered and mixed one with the other. Here every death is felt personally; everyone knows everyone, or at least has heard his name, or has a friend who knows him. It is a land of intensity, of miracles, and of the deepest insecurity. A land where every opinion is broadcast, every action examined; whose destiny is endlessly debated, whose right to exist is constantly challenged. Jerusalem has been destroyed more times than any other city; the people are the most destroyed people in history. The state has fought a constant war of survival for forty-five years, and the people for thousands of years, and still they face insuperable political, military, and moral threats. It is a people that rises and falls together with the evening news. A people desolated and half insane from the Holocaust and the murder of 1,500,000 of its children. A people who have never had a day's peace.[3]

The Jew in his homeland is not the same person he is in Los Angeles, Addis Ababa, Leningrad, or Casablanca. Here the disguises of exile gradually become transparent; personality traits and emotions which had been suppressed or dormant come alive. And what is true of individuals is even more true of the people. A whole people is reemerging with the characteristic energy, strengths, and weaknesses recognizable in the Israelites of the Torah. The landscape of the Torah remains recognizable, especially in the hills and deserts, so that one is able to live in the same spatial dimension as did (do) the ancestors. Here roots expose themselves, recurrence breaks through the surface of daily life.

Israel is the land that "devours its inhabitants" [Lev. 26, 38]; whose problems are so complicated, whose moral dilemmas are so heartbreaking, upon whom the world's judgment is so relentless, that one is spinning in a vortex. There is such *pressure* that many leave every summer just to breathe like human beings. It is a land of fascination and revulsion, of ecstacy and depression. It is said that here bread contains all of the pleasant tastes that exist in the world, and the taste of all of its sorrows. A land that vomits its inhabitants out; a land in which most Jews do not want to live and have never even visited—a land which spawned voluntary diasporas for over twenty-five hundred years. Israel is the land that the Tribes of Israel refused to enter even after the redemption from the slavery of Egypt, even after the revelation of Sinai. It is land that people only want to be buried in. The land of Jewish hopes and of pilgrimage, the land to which Jews have walked thousands of miles to reach; a land of dancing and innumerable songs. Israel is the land that Jews have died for and struggled for and are constantly risking their own and their childrens' lives for. The land of the past, the land that lives day by day and cannot think ahead, the land of the messianic future. This is the highest of the lands and the punished land; the land to which, according to the *Midrash*, Adam was taken after the sin to work its soil. It is the land where everything is mixed and confused; the land where "there is no lack of anything" [Deut. 9].

The rectification of Israel is understood kabbalistically to be a prototype for the rectification of the world. The relation of the Land of Israel to other lands is the analogue to the relation of the soul of Israel to the souls of the other nations. Associated with the *sefirah* of *Malchut*, both the land and the Community of Israel are equated with all reality, and with all humanity. Israel is the only place where all the mitzvot necessary for the total rectification of reality can be performed, where the process of the perfection of souls through the resurrection will culminate. Therefore "Dwelling in the land of Israel weighs equally to all the commandments of the Torah".[4] Only here can a Jew serve the infinite purpose with his whole life, with his every thought, with his every action.[5] This is the place of action, where the truth of Israel and the meaning of its history are revealed. Here there are no disguises and no excuses. If the Jewish people can make it in this land, the world can make it.

2. Seeding

The *Mishnah* lists thirty-nine categories of work which cease on *Shabbat*, each of which is a stage of rectification. These thirty-nine categories are derived from work connected with the construction of the Tabernacle in the desert.[6] The various kinds of labor are listed in the order that they are actually performed. The first eleven stages begin with the working of the land, culminating in the production of the shew bread used in the Tabernacle, the symbol of all sustenance. From this it may be understood that the process of the rectification of reality begins with the land.[7] The first two categories of work, however, appear in reverse order: "The seeding and the ploughing". The process of rectification begins with the act of impregnation: seeding before ploughing (before soil preparation), giving before receiving, action before being.

The primary act is the creation of new potentiality.[8] A person seeds himself into uncertainty, into life—*blindly*, before the ground is prepared, before he is ready. By allowing himself to be false, he explores. This is the archetypal masculine act: purposive, visionary but lacking in being. Action impregnates reality. By the very force of acting, one shapes the world into a womb. The process of "seeding" underlies the Jewish (reversed) approach expressed by the famous dictum, *na'aseh v'nishmah*. Act—and then "hear"; hearing being the sense associated with understanding (*Binah*). *Na'aseh v' nishmah* is the spiritual parallel to the process of scientific experimentation, the process of transcendence.

A transcendent choice is against the ego's security in favor of a spiritual *potential*, a choice to play for higher stakes with life. The purpose of free choice is to explore. Real exploration is possible only through *action*. The deeper one explores life, the deeper one experiences oneself—the more real the infinite becomes. Once the personal ego risk is taken, once there is vulnerability, the universe grows the transcendent act with its own power. Judaism affirms that rich and unexpected rewards ("blessing") flow as long as a person's choice remains fertile. Once the potential of the "seed" is exhausted, a new choice presents itself.

The transcendent process involves progressive stages of *tzimtzumim* or "voids", in which new levels of consciousnesses are born. These periods are likened to the experience of the dormant, rotting seed in the earth. The transition from one state of being to another is not experienced as a direct flowing but as periods of fertility and sterility. (The pathological expression of this movement is manic-depression.) A period of sterility is the inner spiritual womb. The deeper and the more devastating, the more powerful new life rises. This new life is the participation in a higher level of unity.

The secret of coming to the land of Israel is to plant oneself blindly. Returning is not knowing, not doing what one thinks one is doing. Here, knowing oneself is *not* what one was previously conscious of. Maimonides speaks of knowing God through negation: God is not a body, and not a power in a body, etc. This applies as well to knowing oneself in the land. In a letter to his *chassidim* in Europe, Rabbi Abraham of Kolisko wrote:[9]

Everyone who comes to the Sanctuary (the Land of Israel) must be born again in his mother's womb, be suckled again, be a little child again . . . , until he looks directly into the face of the land and his soul is bound up with its soul.

The worker giving himself to the land experiences what the land experiences. Rain sweetens the man as it sweetens the soil;[10] when he builds a terrace in the right place, there is an *uplift*, a jerk, as both he and the land take form. Planting oneself means that everything the land experiences is experienced in oneself—its fertility, its vulnerability. As Rabbi Mendel of Vitebsky wrote, "all the sufferings which we have passed through in these years are the suffering of the land of Israel". With the return of the Zionist pioneers, the will of the land and the will of the pioneers united in a great return to each other.[11] The return is also a return to the people. *All that is said about working the land of Israel applies to living with the Jewish people.*

There is a Garden within the land, within its day-by-day existence. When one is bound up with the soul of the land of Israel and with its people, there are moments, hours, even days when the shells disappear and its infinity is lived. One enters the Garden by becoming the Garden. The Garden that is praise—that is the union of one's inner eternity with the eternal in the Land of Israel and in its people, the Garden that is in all land and in all people.

NOTES

1. In Israel there are over 470 bird species; this is more than the number reported, for example, in larger countries such as the United Kingdom. There are approximately 3000 genera of plants in Israel, 150 of which are endemic. See M. Zohary, *Plants of the Bible* (Cambridge U. Press, 1982), and U. Paz, *The Birds of Israel* (Steimatzky, 1987).

2. *Bereshit Rabbah* 5:7.

3. According to the *Midrash*, on the same night that King Solomon completed the Temple, he married Pharaoh's daughter [*Midrash Raba, Naso* 10, D]. Thus the *Leshem Shevo v'Achlamah* concludes that "in the history of Israel, there has not been even one night of rest" (Part II, p. 26).

For a profound modern understanding of the meaning of Israel, see E. Berkovitz, *Faith After the Holocaust* (Ktav, 1973), Ch. VI.

4. *Sifri, Re'eh* 12:29.

5. A halachic expression of this is the law that if a couple is living outside of Israel, and the wife wants to move into Israel, the husband must listen to her. If not, she is entitled to a divorce.

6. *Shabbat* 49b; 73a.

7. There are two different types of land. The Torah emphasizes that Egypt is watered by the Nile floods, and by the labor of man. In an irrigated land like Egypt, Pharaoh becomes God because there is no faith. Whereas Israel is dependent upon rain. God is the owner of the Land of Israel and He waters the land.

8. The Sages consider the act of seeding to be an expression of faith. The title of the first of the six orders of the *Mishnah* is "Seeds", which is referred to by the

Sages as "Faith" [*Shabbat* 31a]. Faith (*emunah*) is connected to the Hebrew word *man* (the mannah in Sinai), which was described as being like coriander seed falling from the sky.

9. Quoted in M. Buber, *On Zion* (Schocken, 1973), p. 96.

10. Rain is a symbol for union. Rain "pleases the land", and this is expressed in laughter. The land is laughing and "having a good time". "Pleasure" and "land" are closely connected in Hebrew. To please, *leratzot*, is connected to the root for both will (*ratzon*) and land (*eretz*).

11. Thus A. D. Gordon wrote,

The mother *Eretz* Israel, claims your body and life or she claims nothing . . .

Only when you begin to look for something, that something that no Jew can find anywhere else . . . only then will you be competent to do something of essential importance for Israel. (Buber, Ibid., p. 160).

AN OVERVIEW OF THE KABBALISTIC REALITY

This Chapter seeks to present an overview of the kabbalistic understanding of reality in a more systematic and philosophic vein than does the main text. As would be expected, there are various schools with differing emphases and viewpoints in respect to the interpretation of key concepts and details. The view presented is based on the writings of the *Ari* as interpreted by *Chassidism*.

1. The Creation, and the Tzimtzum (Withdrawal; Contraction)

The first act of creation was to bring about space within the undivided Oneness (more precisely, within the transcendent light of Infinity) in which the Cosmos could exist. This primordial space (*challal*) was formed by an act of withdrawal or constriction (*tzimtzum*) of the light into itself—forming a void. Within this vacated space the Creation takes place. The *Ari* describes the process as follows: [1]

> Before all things were created . . . the Supernal light was simple. It filled all existence. There was no empty space which would be space, emptiness or void. Everything was filled with the simple *Or Ain Sof* (transcendent light of Infinity). There was no category of beginning and no category of end. All was one simple undifferentiated Infinite light.
>
> When it arose in His simple Will to create all universes, He constricted His infinite light, distancing it to the sides around a center point, leaving a vacated [spherical] space in the middle of the light of *Ain Sof*. . .
>
> After this constriction (*tzimtzum*) took place . . . there was a place in which all things could be brought into existence (the world of *Atzilut*), created (*Beriyah*), formed (*Yitzirah*), and completed (*Assiyah*). He then drew a simple concentrated ray from the light of Infinity that surrounded the space . . . The upper extremity of this ray touched the light of Infinity that surrounded the space and extended towards its center. It was through this ray, serving as a

conduit, that the (immanent) light of Infinity was brought down and spread into the entire vacated space."

A distinction is drawn between the unchanging being of God (*Atzmut*) which cannot be known and which does not involve the Creation directly, and the Infinite Light (*Or Ain Sof*), which is the manifestation or revelation of God's will. More precisely, God's light emanates in two ways: as transcendent light, which is undifferentiated will that "surrounds all worlds", and as immanent light which "fills all worlds". Immanent light is that aspect of God's will that has been defined, and which manifests as the Creation within the vacated space.[2] The immanent light (*Or Ain Sof HaMemale Col Almin*) is the *inner life force* that fills or pervades all aspects of reality. If the transcendent light is potentiality in God's will, the immanent light expresses its actualization—His "speech", His continuous "speaking" forth of the Creation [Gen. 1]. The transcendent or all-encompassing light (*Or Ain Sof HaSovev Col Almin*) exists equally everywhere, and is considered to be the "higher" light because its undifferentiated nature is more consistent with God's being. Experienced only in the higher levels of consciousness, it is sensed as emanating from the being of God—as the sense of divine exaltation, of the life of all life that pervades existence.

From God's perspective the *tzimtzum* is not real.[3] "He was, He is, He will be . . ." all at the same "instant" above time.[4] If He were to withhold His "speech" and thus destroy the image of the universe, nothing in Him would change. *Chassidism* makes clear, therefore, that the *tzimtzum* in the writings of the *Ari* should not be taken literally as it is impossible to apply a spatial concept to God. The *tzimtzum* is to be understood in a conceptual context which addresses the paradox of the existence of the imperfect, finite world existing within the absolute oneness and perfection of God. Nevertheless, in this paradoxical space—the paradox of monotheism itself—reality takes place.

In the second phase of the Creation, a ray of light entered into the *challal* (Figure 5).[5] The ray is likened to a seed entering the "womb" formed by the *tzimtzum*. (The ray entering the *challal* is the paradigm of the male and female principles.)[6] From this ray of immanent light spiralled ten concentric circles. These are the ten *sefirot* with which God fills all worlds, and which relate to the ten sayings in Genesis 1 ("And God said let there be light . . .", etc.) through which the universe was and continues to be created. As will be discussed below, through a process of numerous such *tzimtzumim* and emanations, light evolves into the reality that is known to ordinary consciousness.

Figure 5   **The Ray of Light of Infinity Entering the Vacated Space of the *Tzimtzum***

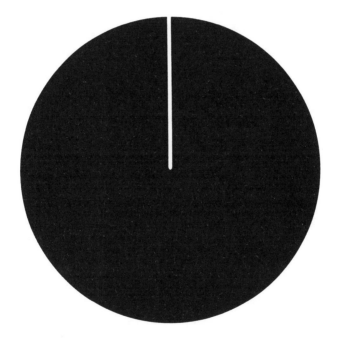

Figure 6   **The Ten *Sefirot* Inter-included One within the Other.**

Diagram composed of the initial letters or the names of each *sefirah* starting with *Keter* and going to *Malchut*. *Yesod* is expressed by the letter *tzadde*.

From Moses Cordevero, *Pardes Rimmonim* (Cracow, 1592).

2. The Five Worlds

The ray of the light of Infinity evolves into ordinary reality through five "Worlds" which express five levels of its progressive "enclothement"; that is, through five basic levels of consciousness. "Higher" and "lower" Worlds refer to the degree the light of Infinity is concealed; a higher World is not in any way "closer" spatially to God than a lower World. Rather, each of the five levels of consciousness is enclothed within the "garment" of the other; each World is the soul or inner-consciousness of the succeeding one. All five Worlds exist one within the other within the other in each moment of consciousness. This principle of inter-inclusion (*hitcalelut*) is considered fundamental to all truth (Fig. 6).

The five levels of enclothement progressively "hide the Face" (God's manifest involvement with the Creation), allowing the lower levels of consciousness to exist without being obliterated. Without garments (forms, images) nothing but light can manifest. (This process is hinted at in the Hebrew word for "world" (*olam*), whose root means "concealment"). The "garment" or form serves both to cover, and to resolve light into form. Each of the five Worlds is identical but at progressively increasing levels of articulation. In an analogous way, consciousness can be considered the outer garment for the soul, and thought the outer garment for consciousness, and speech the garment for thought, and action the garment for speech.

The five Worlds are levels of consciousness; an infinite number of screenings of the immanent light would not result in physical matter which involves the creative power of the transcendent Light. At the lowest levels of consciousness are fantasies, dreams, and even worse dreams. Nevertheless, important *qualitative* differences or jumps exist between the Worlds themselves. This is especially the case between the two higher as compared to the three lower Worlds; and as well, between all the Worlds of consciousness and the physical realm. The World of *Assiyah* (literally "making" or action) is the dimension of ordinary consciousness. The physical world also takes place at this level.[7]

The following simplified example, using five developmental stages[8] involved in building a "house" (the Creation), may illustrate the distinctions between the Worlds: (1) *Adam Kadmon* (Primordial Man):[9] the will to build the house; (2) *Atzilut* (Emanation): the wisdom as to how to build a house; (3) *Briah* (Creation): the general concept of the house, its architectural design; (4) *Yetzirah* (Formation): the building instructions and detailed contruction plan; (5) *Assiyah* (Action, Making): the final building of the house, the actualization of the original will and purpose. The physical world, which also takes place in *Assiyah*, would consitutute the house itself. Thus the lowest of the Worlds, which is day-to-day reality, is a mixture of ordinary consciousness and matter.

The five Worlds may also be thought of as representing five levels of oscillation.[10] Just as the conversion of energy into matter absorbs and re-organizes energy in a new form, in each World light is reorganized into five *partzufim* (personifications, power centers). Each of the five *partzufim* is in turn, organized into ten *sefirot* which reflect the light "down" into ever more defined forms. The World of *Assiyah* is the dimension of greatest intensity and definition. Physics explains that the greater the intensity of particle binding that forms physical objects, the greater the hardness or concreteness of materials. Continuing the analogy, the intensity or "coarseness" acts as the barrier to perception of the inner divinity. Thus Kabbalah uses the terms "shells", and "garments" when speaking of the nature of ordinary reality. In meditation or prayer, for example, when brain waves change frequency, the mind is able to pass through its own shells into the higher Worlds of consciousness. The higher or deeper one reaches, the more the oscillation barrier becomes subtle and diaphanous. There is more light and less form, until a level is reached in direct mystical experience where the light is too strong to be held in the structure of the mind.

3. The Tree of Life, the Ten Sefirot

The sefirotic system is the basic kabbalistic framework and language through which reality is perceived. In each World there are ten *sefirot*, expressing the same ten aspects or potentials of the light of *Ain Sof* at that particular level of emanation.[11] The *sefirot* are powers or potentialities inherent within the Infinite light which traverse from infinity to the finite creation. (The universe described by the *sefirot* is relative to, and is affected by, the viewer, as explained in relativity theory and in quantum physics.) The two infinity points of the microcosm and the macrocosm unite in their one genesis, the primordial *tzimtzum*. The sefirotic structure and processes apply both to consciousness and to that of the physical world. For example, the human body, the realms of the metals, liquids, colors, the structure of a tree, etc. can be expressed and inter-related sefirotically. A man who looks into his psyche sees the same universal structures and processes that are active in the physical world. This is the basis for the power of man to understand the Cosmos and to achieve communion with all levels of existence.

In the view of Kabbalah, therefore, the human psyche is a hologram in the holographic universe.[12] In the holographic structure of the *sefirot*, each part is in the whole, and the whole is in each part. Each *sefirah* is

Figure 7 **The Ten Sefirot & Their Inner Life Force or Experience**

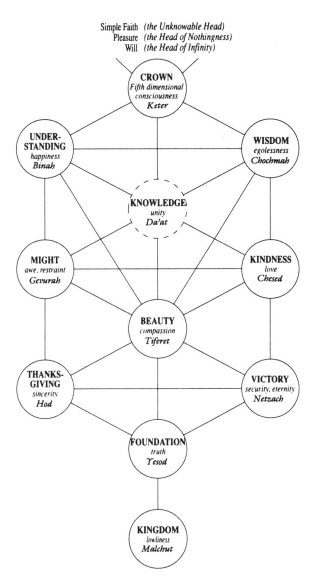

Figure 8　**The Holographic Structure of the** *Sefirot*

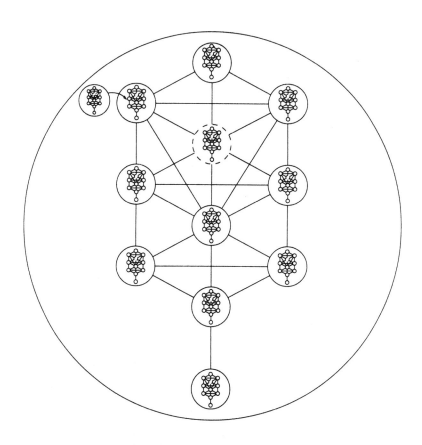

Figure 9   The Creative Dynamic of the *Sefirot* in the Order of
Their Emanation

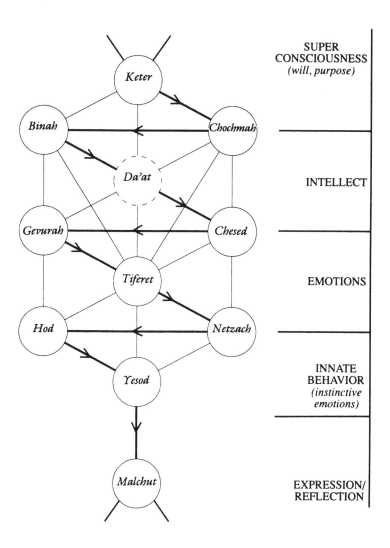

composed of ten sub-*sefirot*, and each sub-*sefirah* is a compound of ten sub-sub-*sefirot* ad infinitum (Figure 8). Each of the ten *sefirot* is meaningful only in relation to its opposite, to each of the other *sefirot*, and in relation to the whole. This is the function of the twenty-two lines of relationship which define the flow within the whole configuration. The structure of the *sefirot* is based on three flow lines: left-right-center (Figures 7, 9). The right side is associated with expansion and unity, the basic male principle. The left side is associated with form, concentration, and individualization—the basic female principle. The center line expresses the harmonization or synergistic effect between the two opposite forces at each level. The power of the middle line is to balance and to synergistically resolve opposites. It is through the center that the divine purpose moves down through all levels in a process of progressive actualization.[13]

At the same time that the *sefirot* are dimensions or qualities of the divine will, they are also vessels which receive the light from the higher Worlds, and in turn reflect light "down". (The concept of giving is related to "light", while that of receiving is related to "vessel".) The light of Infinity emanating through the *sefirot* in each of the five Worlds, may be thought of as passing through a series of prisms which break the light into ten potent "colors" or creative forces. The five Worlds represent five major levels or stages at which the process repeats itself: a prism within a prism within a prism, etc.—progressively absorbing (concealing) but at the same time resolving and defining the light. In turn, each *sefirah* is itself a particular facet of the prism, breaking the light into the ten sub-colors and then into a hundred sub-sub-colors, and then into a thousand sub-sub-sub colors or manifestations, etc. (Figure 8). Through this ever-changing and infinitely complex play of the forces of the ten *sefirot*, the images of reality are formed.

4. The Breaking of the Vessels

The primordial "catastrophe" called the Breaking of the Vessels (*Shevirat HaKeilim*), and the subsequent restoration of the cosmic order (the World of *Tikkun*, Rectification), constitute the second stage of creation following the *tzimtzum*. The Breaking of the Vessels is alluded to in the *Midrash* which states that God created universes and destroyed them.[14] As well, it is based on the Zoharic account of the destruction of primordial worlds hinted at in the biblical reference to the death of seven of the eight kings who "reigned in the land of Edom before any king reigned over the children of Israel" [Gen. 36].

Kabbalah interprets the death of the primordial Kings of Edom as referring to the previous order in which the forces of *Gevurah* ("stern judgment") were predominant. Edom signifies the realm of *Gevurah* without the mediation of *Chesed* (benevolence) or *Tiferet* (compassion). In this primordial stage of creation following the *tzimtzum*, the light of *Ain Sof* emanated in the form of a line of ten "points" which became the primitive vessels of the World of *Tohu* (Primordial Chaos).[15] Each of these proto-*sefirot* was isolated with no connection to the other sefirotic points. When the power of the light of *Ain Sof* emanated into these "primitive" vessels, the highest three *sefirot* were able to receive and hold the revelation (although with some damage) but the next seven shattered because they were isolated "kings" unable to interact to form a whole. The Breaking of the Vessels is the "death" of the the seven kings of Edom, which refers to the breaking of each of the lower seven *sefirot* issuing from *Binah* (the Higher Mother).

After the breaking, the main stream of light reascended to its origin. The remaining light (the "sparks") was trapped in the fragmented vessels which fell to their "grave", the "place" of the three lower Worlds. (As the *Zohar* explains, something is said to have died when it leaves its true level and descends to a lower level of existence.)[16] As the fragments of these vessels "fell" further, they broke into an ever-increasing number of images. This process continued through the Lower Worlds, until the coarsest (the most articulated) fell into what is now our world (the World of *Assiyah*) and its physical counterpart, the world of matter. In this respect, a rock or tree may be thought of as an image (a fragment of the fallen vessel) which obscures an inner spark of the immanent light of Infinity.[17] The form and properties of the "rock" are determined by the inner spark which fell from a corresponding but more abstract manifestation of the "rock" in a higher World; the physical material is most basically the creation of the transcendent light.

God rectified the universe (the World of *Tikkun*) but retained its fragmented structure (See below, sect. 6). The *Ari* explains, for example, that the light originally intended to be in the vessel of *Chesed* in the World of *Atzilut* fell to the level of *Yesod* of *Atzilut*. The light's corresponding vessel, however, fell to the *sefirah* of *Binah* in the next lower World of *Briah*. In kabbalistic terms, this is what is meant by the broken world. In other words, desires and aspirations exist at a lower level than do their true fulfillment. Forms are cruder than their ideal and cannot hold their intended content. It is as if the mind were a ten-storey building in the aftermath of an earthquake. The foundations have sunk into the earth. The upper three stories remain damaged but intact while the next seven stories have crashed through the ceilings of lower floors. As will be discussed below, the purpose of man is to rectify (unify, raise, restore, heal) the discrepancy between the forms of this world and their intended energies.

5. Evil and Free Choice

With the concealment of the divine in the forms of reality, the world as we know it was established:

> I am the Lord, and there is none else;
> I form the light and create darkness;
> I make peace and create evil . . . [Isa. 45:6-7]

Man is forced to exist in the midst of the disharmony of a broken world, a disharmony between energy and its proper forms, between aspiration and the possibilities of fulfillment, between the drive to unify with God and His hiddenness. This brokenness and confusion is a fundamental source of concealment beyond that of the process of creation itself. Our reality is God's choice which He continuously recreates:

> Against your will you were formed, and against your will you were born, against your will you live, against your will you die, and against your will you [. . . will be judged]. [Sayings of the Fathers 4:22.]

Thus the problem of evil is rooted in the most fundamental questions: Why did God create man? What divine benevolence or "experiment" must be created at the price of even one child's suffering?

From the human point of view, in the realm of ordinary consciousness created by the *tzimtzum*, God's presence is not felt.[18] In the void, as it were, God does not exist. The *Baal Shem Tov* interprets the phrase, "And I will hide the hiding of My face from you" (Deut. 31:18), as meaning that there is a double hiddenness—the fact that God's face is hidden is itself hidden. Those who penetrate to the emptiness and meaninglessness of life reach a real place but it is not the ultimate place. Those who choose to break through their own consciousness and to penetrate beyond the non-existence of God will find Him.[19] In the higher levels of consciousness, God's goodness and pure love are invariably revealed; this is the ultimate human answer, beyond philosophy, beyond evil. Thus Judaism teaches that God created the universe for the purpose of bestowing His good on man, and that this highest good is the direct experience of the divine.

God "hides His face", both from the Creation that it may exist, and from those who suffer, that man may exist. Tolerance of evil is the continuation of the primordial *tzimtzum* which creates the space for existence itself. God's self-restraint opens the realm of free choice, the realm of the human. It is free will which defines man as being created in the image of God [Gen. 1:27]. The precondition for the existence of free will is the equal possibility that God is not present.[20] To the extent that God interferes he degrades the idea of man. The innocent who suffer pay the price for this freedom.[21] Nevertheless, it is through the possibility of evil that the realm of man's dominion expands.[22] Nevertheless we pray that He will intervene, that He will take away or reduce our freedom.

Man's choice and the potential for evil were "born" together, as the twins Jacob and Esau were born from the same womb. Evil is called the "other side" (*sitra achra*), indicating that for every potentiality on the side of good there exists a counter-potential on the side of evil.[23] Evil, however, is defined relatively as the concealment of light, or as separated self-consciousness. The difference between good and evil is the extent to which the divine is revealed. Evil is the manifestation of ignorance, or of constricted consciousness. The possibility of evil manifests to the extent that man's consciousness of God is suppressed or diverted to "idols"; good manifests to the extent the infinite unity is revealed. Because of the inner divine spark, evil is never absolute or irredeemable. Kabbalah teaches, therefore, that the power of good is greater than the potential power of evil. Evil's ultimate opposite, however, is peace (*shalom*) in which all opposites are resolved. Because evil has no independent existence, it is seen as a parasitic or cancerous process which "sucks" on the spark of the infinite life it conceals. Just as an effective lie must be based on a spark of truth, so evil must be pursued in the name of good.

On the personal level, the effect of evil or sin is to separate or exile a person from the source of his true life. The "punishment" for evil is everdeepening isolation. Nevertheless, there is no such thing as a purely private sin or evil act, just as there is no private, isolated good. By strengthening the power of concealment, each evil action corrupts mankind as a whole and deepens the exile of the entire Creation.

6. The Rectification of Reality (Tikkun)

After the Breaking of the Vessels, God established a new order using the powers of *Chesed* (loving kindness) and *Tiferet* (harmonization). The new cosmic order is called the World of Rectification (*Tikkun*). Genesis 1:2, "and the world was *tohu* and *vohu* . . .", is interpreted as referring to the previous World of *Tohu*; and Genesis 1:3, "Let there be light and there was light . . .", as referring to the World of *Tikkun*. The primordial "breakage" resulted from the fact that the proto-*sefirot* were independent powers (a line of separate "points") which did not exhibit the mutuality and harmony that characterize a stable whole. In the World of *Tikkun*, the ten *sefirot* in each of the five Worlds are arranged into five *partzufim* (literally, "faces"; personifications, power centers) which constitute stable, holistic vessels for the light of Infinity.[24] The World of *Tikkun*, however, is primarily related to the rectified world of *Atzilut*. The world of man and nature (*Assiyah*) remains displaced and broken; it is a world whose images are the fallen images of *Tohu*. The process of *tikkun* is to ultimately raise this World and the lower Worlds to the highest spiritual World of *Atzilut*, which is pure God-consciousness.

All created as well as inanimate beings such as stones, water, or earth possess a soul and the divine life force.[25] As in man, the primary desire in all of nature is to reunite with the infinite, to return to the primordial singularity. When Adam fell, nature fell with him [Gen. 3:17-19]; the land became less fertile, the animals began to hunt each other, disease erupted. The physical world may be lifted up or returned by two basic processes. A physical object may be involved either directly in a formal *mitzvah* or in any other act of holiness. For example, eating with the proper blessings, etc., raises the sparks captured in the specific plant or slaughtered animal. The spark of divinity within the food is consumed, metamorphosed, and then rises through enlightened human consciousness and action to the infinite. Nature may also be rectified through man's communion. Instead of being an object of worship, nature, natural beauty and pure landscape open man's awareness to their mutual creator. Here the sparks of light captured in the forms of nature are "absorbed" directly into human consciousness. As the *Baal Shem Tov* taught:

> Whenever you look at a physical thing, you should contemplate that you are looking at the immanent Divine Presence. In this manner, you serve God through smallness (your own physicality).[26]

Nature is an active partner in her own return (*tshuvah*); man and the physical world, which fell together, raise themselves together.[27]

The fallen or broken nature of the world is expressed by the concept of the *Shechinah* (God's immanence) in Exile, exile in a world that does not perceive the divine reality. The exile of Israel among the nations is the analogue in history to the Exile of the *Shechinah*. The "ingathering of the exiles of Israel" on the historical plane is the analogue of the uplifting of all the fallen sparks from among the shells of reality.[28] In the course of history, the process of *tikkun* has progressed but has also retreated. There have been three primary "breakings" or exiles: the cosmic or primordial Breaking of the Vessels, the Sin of Adam, and the Exile of Israel. Each of these primal breakings is the analogue of the others on a different level of reality: the physical world, the world of human relations, and the spiritual world respectively. Sparks captured in physical reality are considered the most external; those whose source is the Sin of Adam, and which are captured in the world of human psychological and social relations, are more internal; and sparks whose source is the Exile of Israel (the sins of Israel), which are captured in the shells which surround or obscure religious consciousness, are the deepest and therefore the most difficult to liberate.[29]

The Fall of Adam corresponded to the fall into, and the "mixing" of, our World of *Assiyah* (which in its rectified form is a purely spiritual world), with the physical world. In the psyche, the Fall expresses the mixing of evil (doubt, misdirected desire, etc.) into the processes of consciousness. A result of the Fall is that man can never be certain as to the objectivity of his perception, nor as to the purity of his desires. In the teachings of Judaism, the rectification of the Fall is through the revelation at Mt. Sinai. Because of its divine source, the Torah by definition is a revelation of objective knowledge which enables a person to transcend the subjective human state.

Action that expands consciousness, that leads towards the revelation of the unity of all existence in God, is rectifying.[30] Action that reinforces illusion or idol worship by denying the reality of the infinite is destructive; if it is done deliberately it is evil. No action is meaningless or without effect. Each man has a special purpose or life's work which is the major area of his *tikkun*; this work, in turn, defines his true identity. The perfection of the individual is a necessary prerequisite for the perfection of existence as a whole. Therefore Judaism affirms that the world was created for the sake of each person. As each man's consciousness is the analogue of all of humanity and of the physical universe, to the extent that he is able to achieve purity of consciousness, all existence is illuminated.

NOTES

1. *Etz Chaim* 1:1:2 as translated in Kaplan, *Innerspace* (Moznaim, 1990), p. 120.

2. *Zohar* 3:225a. Rabbi A. Steinsaltz comments:

> "Encompassing Light" and "Pervading Light" are intended to describe modes of influence on reality as well as angles of perception, the way the ultimate cause works. Indeed, they are really technical terms serving as diagrams or tools. . . . Light that is shed on reality from outside and beyond, and not from within itself, is not to be grasped; . . . .

We, therefore, call (it.) that which encompasses or surrounds us. . . ." (*The Long Shorter Way* (Aronson, 1988), pp. 326-327.

3. *Sha'ar HaYichud V'HaEmunah*, Ch. 7.

4. From the *"Adon Olam"* prayer (Master of the World), attributed to Solomon Ibn Gabirol (11th century).

5. As the ray of light entered the *challal*, it divided into its inner and outer dimensions. This process or dynamic (of inner and outer, upper and lower, transcendent and immanent) is repeated and manifests in a different perspective at every level of existence.

It is further taught that within the *challal*, there remained an "impression" (*reshimu*) of the transcendent light. The manifestation of this "impression" could be likened to that of the background radiation thought to originate in the Big Bang, and which reaches earth from every direction equally.

6. In terms of the mind, the concept of *tzimtzum* applies as between *Keter* (*ayin*; nothingness) and *Chochmah* (the flash of insight), which is the first manifestation of undifferentiated consciousness.

7. See Luzzatto, *The Way of God* (Feldheim, 1981), trans. by A. Kaplan, pp. 177-183. The physical world encloses the two lowest levels of consciousness, *Malchut* and *Yesod of Assiyah*.

8. The idea of development may be misleading. All the Worlds of consciousness come into existence at once "as soon as" God's will arises. Space-time comes into existence with self-consciousness in the three lower Worlds. More precisely, at the highest point (*Keter*) in the World of *Briah*, time and space are condensed into a single point from which they expand into the lower Worlds like a pyramid. For example, a period of fifteen years in our World (*Assiyah*) may be only a moment in the consciousness of the World of *Yetzirah*. Perhaps this can be analogized to the phenomenon of time dilation in which, as a person approaches the speed of light in a hypothetical space vehicle, time slows until at the speed of light there is no time. In our case, approaching the speed of light may be likened to the ascent or penetration of the Worlds of consciousness towards the point of infinity.

9. Because *Adam Kadmon* is a World without vessels, it is sometimes not categorized separately in many books of Kabbalah, in which case only four Worlds are treated.

10. Traditionally, kabbalists have sought in the supreme name of God, Y-H-V-H (generally called *Ha Shem*, the Name)—the basic pattern and process of creation. These five levels, for example, correspond in the following way:

NAME	WORLD	LEVEL OF SOUL	TORAH INTERPRETATION ("*Pardes*")
Tip of Yud	*Adam Kadmon* (*Keter*)	*Yechida* (single one); (divine spark of being)	Messianic revelation
Yud	*Atzilut* (*Chochmah*)	*Chayah* (life force)	Secret, mystical (Kabbalah)
Heh	*Briah* (*Binah*)	*Neshamah* (consciousness)	Verbal analogies, allegory

Vav	*Yetzirah*	*Ruach* (spirit)	Hints, textual
	(*Chesed-Yesod*)		allusions
Heh	*Assiyah* (*Malchut*)	*Nefesh* (soul)	Literal, plain
			meaning of text

The concept of the ten *sefirot* is first mentioned in the ancient *Sefer Yetzirah*. The word *sefirah* has many interpretations as to its derivation: the word for number, "sapphire", or the verb "to tell". Various manifestations and principles of the *sefirot* are also referred to by other terms suitable to the context: lights, pillars, levels, colors, garments, firmaments, crowns, kings, faces, sources, aspects, etc.

When *Keter* is included as a *sefirah* (some exclude it as a *sefirah* because it is super-consciousness in nature), *Da'at* is omitted, and visa versa (Figure 7). This depends on the context; *Keter* is the unconscious, while *Da'at* is the conscious manifestation of *Keter*. As to the Three Heads of *Keter*, see *Zohar* 3:288a; *Sod HaShem Lireav*, p. 33ff.

12. See in general, K. Wilber (ed.), *The Holographic Paradigm* (Shambala, 1985).

13. The drive to *actualize* is in the middle line which culminates in *Yesod* (Truth), and then manifests in reality (*Malchut*). At the level of Mind, the actualization of the mind is to know (*Da'at*); at the level of the Emotions or the heart, actualization is empathy (*Tiferet*). At the level of the direct emotions which direct behavior, actualization is procreation, self-truth, or the "fulfillment of one's promise"—all associated with *Yesod*. For a useful discussion of the *sefirot*, see *The Bahir* (Weiser, 1979), trans. A. Kaplan, pp. 104-107.

14. *Bereshit Rabbah* 3:9; *Shabbat* 55a. See further, *The Bahir*; Ibid., pp. 88-91.

15. The word *Tohu* comes from the root meaning "confounded". When a person is confounded it means that he is perceiving an idea that his mind cannot hold. Similarly, the vessels of *Tohu* received the light of Infinity that they could not contain. Just as confusion and confoundment shatter the thought process, so the vessels were shattered. Kaplan, *Innerspace*; Ibid., p. 80.

According to the *Ari*, the three highest levels of consciousness were/are damaged but did not shatter: *Keter* was blemished, *Chochmah* was shocked and affected, and *Binah* fell but did not shatter.

Tohu was the primordial level of the World of *Atzilut*. The "roots" of all that exists in our world are from the World of *Tohu*. See further, Kaplan, Ibid., Ch. 10.

16. *Zohar* 3:135b.

17. Although the forms of the physical world are dependent upon the nature of the human brain and the way it perceives phenomena, they are not merely figments of the mind. In the Biblical account of Creation, physical reality was created before the birth of Adam.

18. The vacuum created by the *tzimtzum* is not entirely filled by the Creation in its midst. The surrounding emptiness, as it were, is a sphere of separation between the Creation and unrevealed potential or undifferentiated will of God. This emptiness may be perceived as God's nonexistence.

19. Rabbi Eleazer said: "Since the day of the destruction of the Temple, a wall of iron separates Israel from her Father in Heaven". *T. B. Berachot* 32b.

20. In this regard the Talmud states: "All is in the hands of Heaven except for the fear of Heaven". The existence of free will necessitates that it be rational to understand the Creation and the course of history without awareness of or reference to God's providence. To the Jewish understanding, however, the one exception is the enduring reality of the Jewish people through the 3500 years of its history. The history of Israel is considered inexplicable in terms of the historical processes of military power, economics, land rootedness, etc. This is the meaning of Isaiah:

> You are My witnesses, said the Eternal,
> and my servant whom I have chosen;
> That you may know and believe Me, and
> understand
> That I am He . . . [Isaiah 43:10]

To which the Rabbis add: "If you (Israel) are my witnesses, I am God; if you do not witness, I am, as it were, not God".

The idea of Israel as God's witness in history is one of the profound meanings of the idea of the chosen people. Thus the Nazi war against the Jews, as even they understood it and which underlay their metaphysical hatred, was a war against the witnessing of the divine in history. They sought to destroy the Jews as human beings, to reduce Jews to living deadmen. The living deadman of a Godless world, and the servant-angel of the openly revealed God, are the opposing images of man without free will.

21. God's compassion extends also to those who commit evil, to those who choose against Him. Thus according to the Midrash, at the time of the drowning of the Egyptians in the Red Sea, the angels in heaven were preparing to chant their daily hymn of praise to the Almighty. God silenced them: "The works of my hands are drowning in the sea and you sing my praises!"

22. A recent stimulating study from a philosophic perspective is D. Birnbaum, God and Evil (Ktav, 1989). This work, along with those of E. Fackenheim, are recommended to those seeking to explore more deeply the problem of theodicy from a Jewish philosophic perspective. Birnbaum sums up his theodicy as follows (p. 54):

1. The purpose of man is to quest for his potential—spiritual and other.

2. The greater man's freedom, the greater his ability to attain his potential.

3. Freedom requires privacy, responsibility, and selfhood.

4. In order to yield greater freedom . . . , God has contracted His here-and-now consciousness, in correlation to mankind's ascent in knowledge [and possibly consciousness].

5. With the Divine consciousness increasingly contracted . . . , man is increasingly forced to confront evil on his own.

For a moving and relevant treatment of the problem of the impact of the Holocaust upon faith, see E. Berkovits, Faith After the Holocaust (Ktav, 1973).

23. *Zohar* 3:47b.

24. There are five basic configurations (*partzufim*) in each World (each *partzuf* contains ten *sefirot*): *Arich Anpin* (*Keter*); *Abba* (Father; *Chochmah*); *Ima* (Mother; *Binah*); *Zeir Anpin* (the six *Midot*); and *Nukva d'Zeir Anpin* (*Malchut*, the feminine aspect of the *Midot*, usually called the *Shechinah*). This order of *partzufim* represents the rectified nature and structure of reality.

More precisely, the *sefirah* of *Keter* is divided into two *partzufim*. The inner *partzuf* is *Atik Yomin* (the Ancient of Days); the outer *partzuf* is *Arich Anpin* (The Long Countenance or Face).

25. *Etz Chaim* 39:3. *Sha'ar HaYichud V'Emmunah*, Ch. 1. Every living creature possesses a spark of Messiah. *Maor Enaim, Pinchas*, in the name of the *Baal Shem Tov; Likutei Sichot*.

26. *Tzava'ath HaRivash*, pp. 233, 234; Kaplan, *The Light Beyond* (Moznaim, 1981), p. 32.

27. The relation of man to nature, symbolized by the relation of the Jew to the Land of Israel, is governed by very strict laws which preserve the land against exploitation and pollution. Deeper than this, the land's separate moral being is recognized, and is even given precedence in the case that man "defiles" it. Thus the exile of Israel is specifically attributed to the people's failure to give the land its seventh year of rest (*shmittah*); as a result, the land vomited them out.

28. *Etz Chaim, Sha'ar* 26, Ch. 2; *Mevo Shearim, Sha'ar*, Part 1, Ch. 2. The name *Shechinah* is derived from the Biblical phrase, "that I may dwell (*shachanti*) among them" [Exod. 25:8]. See further, Steinsaltz, *The Long Shorter Way*, Ibid., Ch. 52.

29. The Jerusalem Talmud says that if the Jewish people would keep two *Shabbats*, the Messiah would come. The Babylonian Talmud says, even if Israel kept one *Shabbat*. Organized mystical action to bring the Messiah was the focus of much of the kabbalistic activity of the *Ari* and his circle in Safed in the 16th century. The influence of Kabbalah on messianic action continues today.

30. Not all unifications, however, "sew" the world together. "Couplings" must be correct both in terms of intention, substance, and timing. (Thus according to the *Midrash*, Adam's sin was in not waiting for the proper time of *Shabbat* to have relations with Eve.) A union of two persons, ideas, or images must further the purpose of the universe, otherwise it adds further confusion or adulteration.

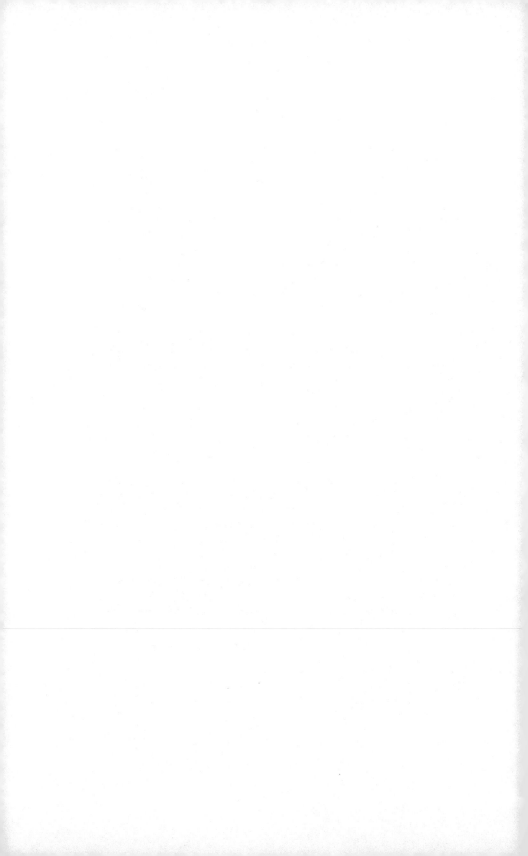

Desire for White

I

PREFACE

Everything, its open mouth
lipless

its gaze cloudless—
everything, its one desire

soundless
desire, of the inner colors of white

1

From your side
light doesn't die

only forms of light
tiny screams like isolated stars,

from your side
it is simple—

no one is lost
nothing can be lost

emerging from light
in the focusing of light

union resolves into the separation

of a man turning in a room
his eyes wide with meditation

appearing as you disappear,
in the closing aperture
death appears

Turning against you

for what you let happen
for what is human,
against you

to the point
no point is left

not burned through by bitterness
to its emptiness

nothing we have done
not purified
not atoned for

by pyramids of children,

to the point
there is no point
left without you

2

Everything that happens
is you

everything human

is a gift to yourself,
a sacrifice

to yourself,

my mouth
is the
prism

for your silence
for your absence

for my life made of death

The eyelids are cut from my eyes—

I wait to become
what will happen

what you want,

I am yours
your boy
your toy

my voice scraping through a hole

is your wind
your speech

3

The shell
is form—

is the dome
the skull

is the density of nothingness,
its intensity

is this thought
a wind hiding silence

Silence that is your

idea of time
your sense of space

that is every direction's disappearance
your face's disappearance

into non-existence
into betrayal,

that is your choice
of our choice

between losses,

choice that must fail
iron in it
agony

until there is no choice
except to find

the nothingness
of your face

that alone fills
space's dome
time's skull

that becomes silence
that becomes water
that is beauty,

that fills why
that fills all but why

4

Just to breathe is pleasure—

we know when pain ceases
all we want is to live, live

everything
is outlined with it—

you sculpt with death

It would have been better
not to be born

that's what life wants,

not to form
not to want

It's good to be very young—

my sons
are mine

and I am theirs'
as you are mine,

and I am yours
as they are mine

because they are helpless
I am all they have

because of death
you are all I have

5

In the opening of the psyche
by the mind itself

so much delicate destruction
is involved
dissolving its reality

too much for a man
grasping its broken pieces

The world is
too good
too evil

too sexual

to do what you want,

to reveal your existence
hidden in cries against your injustice,

hidden in trenches
in freedom

6

After death

the sun
opens wordless

like a command it is quiet

Pyres are burning prisms

rain falling—
peaceful as it was
Spring won't be prevented

flowers like excited eyes glint in mud
The ground underfoot virulent

II
PREFACE

To the wound's edge
to the white sapphire breath

the heart stopped
the truth

the dying inhale
they hear

7

High mountain walls—
blossom all across the sky
blind in night's sun

gnarled trunk twists darkness,
endless branches revolve—

Night ripening into earth
its fruit, eyes

taste of death

8

The mountains rise
in night
into night

from the capture
the body dies into
from its silhouette of faces,

seeds rise
in color
into savour

abstract to beauty
attract escape from curvature
from the conservation of energy,

at the same time
fighting to reappear
offering to disappear

The mountains rise
in the throat
into voice

in the return of creation
as self-reflection,
its way out

in a man's spiral
his spiraling

the opening of the aperture
wider than structure—

the sucking out of death
the inhaling breath
of who you are

9

Now close as I must be at death

head forcing back
in the arch of singing

in falling darkness

turning inside out

the sudden woman of myself
the yielding of all I am

to coming light

the beginning
open towards me

      ★   ★   ★

  Hold me

  hold me
  longer

  who is yours
  who you sent away

curving me
arching me
back

in waves
without resistance

as arching is singing
as singing is desiring

Singing stopped
in the night room

In new absence,

in happiness
for all of us

my head white radiance
a skull of radiance

the crown of all of us

10

Your eyes flower, full of seed
eyes in a garden walled by cypress trees

my beard brushes the flow of your back
I hold the curve of your night waist,
we sleep in the forms of hand-held dancing
in the forms of walking over lands

Now your look does not leave its garden
does not fall,
my eyes open between your black eyelids
there is fragrance of seed, of the intense marriage

11

for Susan

Two flights—

two black kites
rise in
spirals,

two faces
in sun
in shadow,

to penetrate
to yield
in gyres

of centrifugal forces,

four sons in orbit
as we ourselves orbit
around the vortex,

a woman
and her man,
as they get older
as they reach higher
as far as desire reaches

Knowing you is being drawn
into my darkness—
at its precipice

the rise of your aspiration
forces me,
what you want from me
what you want for me—

as silence forms the sky
as the spiral forms in my silence
I am with you
dying with you
in love with you

12

The still reflection
of a tall wading bird,
I hardly hold you
in water—

you recline as the light
of violet, lilac, purple descends mountains,
obliterates the mountains—

The steppe eagles spiraling north
are a scarf of black stars wrapping your face,
birds rose and gold spark through reeds
the way I can hardly know you—
reeds whose plumes are cypresses
wheat whose sound is young reeds

palm trees fan the way I want to open you

My hands are rough crumbling earth
that are bruising you—

trying to hold light
my hands fissure

13
In the absence
that is life's woman

each star
each rock

each instant
is expectation,

even death moves towards you
its palms stretching towards you

Life that you force away—

who every instant
you force into existence

in the space-time
of your absence

in your purpose
that is your absence,
misses you—

she would forget everything
leave everyone

her bird voices
her gold, silver voices—

leave the sun a whirlpool in the sky

in the concentration
of the lovers' union

in the consummation
of their one desire

through worlds
of hiding
of light *playing*

through endless
masks and shells,

kiss us—

kiss us who miss you
who expect you

kiss our brains
our fingers
our deserts

kiss the night
kiss the sun light

with lightning

with life that will not return us
the white kisses of your mouth

The Poetry of
Allen Afterman

The Maze Rose

Purple Adam

In the Other

Certain of these poems were re-spaced by Stanley Moss. Beyond
that there is no change in the original text.

The Maze Rose

Poems 1970-1973

ROSE

To live the special truth within is a terrible
      algebra of secret symbols and transubstantiation;
of levels and layers—a syllogism with phases
      of moons and weather. It is a truth

of flesh, flesh undulating within confines of skin.
      It is the logic of growth, and a proof for zero.
My body is made of this and is my final barrier.
      We are each as true as the other, and unfold.

Whatever I name I know dies, and is subsumed;
      I seek still the secrets which elude me.
I know a few questions only.
      I know the one living course within me.

I am the rose which cannot free itself,
      which can free only small blood buds. Pick me.
A bee within is waiting. I am pressed
      in spiral—flight! flight to escape.

A petal unfolds, and I am trapped more completely.

                                                                        1972

THE FORESTS ARE ON FIRE

My forests are on fire with the laughter of women;
their eyes scurry like glowing beetles in a log on fire.
We dance in a coven of flaming leaves
about the laurel of their hair.
I am as potent to them
as a half-corona tossed on the street,
yet they divert themselves. I lie between their wide-
stretched legs like a broken tree,
and yet they moan. I am their hero
by necessity, by amusement.
Ha! they laugh, cheri. I say sweetie pie plum.

136

In their spring of light and sharp shade,
in their uninhabited eyes I seek
space of an endless sapphire I can live.
And don't they smell of garlic snails
and badly vented toilets; and don't they
have rocky teeth and sand for gums? They do.
They are mine by desperation.

This in the marvelous maze rose—through moist
dank alleys of rose—through to sudden
bursting rooms of laughter and stained glass light;
deeper and deeper in spirals of the flower,
and of leaving rooms exhausted—
this small ant with pretensions toward the heart.
But if I couldn't dive, how would I live
through this life of details
and inter-personal relations—
knowing they exist, those few
graced chambers in the heart of stained glass.

1973

AS A BULB DIMS OTHERS

Maybe we spent, or burned,
their thinner lives—
as a bulb dims others
their faces shadowed;

what was real, we created,
infusing the ordinary with power,
packing it—
until like a new born sun
it bloomed into light.
Moments. Moments so intense,
like a beacon they jutted out:
drew all life
as a jewel does light.

Who you were in particular,
I don't know. Someone pulled you away
without your resistance.

I was handed a drink, and engaged
in conversation...

those nearest us, with vengeance,
moved to recover.

1971

WITH SOLITUDE AND PINS

Only weeks ago I thought I'd gotten somewhere
(with solitude and pins), where there's no wanting.
I thought of myself as a shimmering glass ball,
strong enough to withstand my needing you,
or any other love—that I was disappearing;

and if everything came of itself, if I could just
stand passive and draw love to me,
I would accept what was offered—
and no more.

Like black-jack, cards threw themselves at me, confirming me,
pushing me toward the chance of loving you. And again
in what seemed soft erupting buds, my flesh
returned and covered me gradually. It pulled me in,
held me (my clarity), consumed me
by half completing...
I began to lie in the usual way—
with honesty and confession—in order to have you,
to draw you around me completely. And again, you left me.

1971

LETTER TO MEG

Meg, I envy you, craving women as well.
Your eyes must burn the whole time,
your skin must always be moist;
no matter where you turn, there's possibility.

With you as we walk, Meg,
I see you making love to every girl that passes by.
I feel like stopping them for you, and opening their blouse.
...When you spread a woman's thighs all lips part together;
you know exactly her movement, her whispers,
her nails curling your hair...

Meg, your tongue, the fingernail you draw
down a woman's back is pure skin;
your finger darting in her lips is skin:
no fertility, but the softest skin:
the most powerful.

Sometimes I wish my tongue was yours.
I wish my belly was as smooth and clear,
my breasts as rich;
I wish I could be your smile,
and the experience of your knowing lips.
Sometimes, Meg, I wish we lived in a pornographic
slide: the three of us Meg, just about to come.

                                                    1970

LETTER TO CLAIR

I wonder if you know that your
light still clings to my skin like old rain; that
it dissipates everything into a vague glow.
I wonder if you felt the disappearance
of me near you. Do you know
I can't picture your face, or your eyes,
which never looked at me but once in bed.

After we made love, you know, I couldn't tell
when it began and when it ended: it was the same
to me as the times I held your hand or your belt;
it was the same one long moment which eased
into the skin of the whole night—
and it seemed we were drawn into a circle closing.
          You were the feel of white powder falling through my
body
          like a shawl of thinnest lace
          sliding gently down the air.

I wonder if you know, Clair, when I say your name
I don't want to know it,
that I am fighting to widen my eyes, to move you
back into the landscape with the others. Who are you anyway?

1971

LETTER TO S THIS MORNING

How are you
black aqua face; you
and your sharp corners?
How are your sharp white bones,
sticking
from water like debris? Huh.
O you are so beautiful.
Beautiful
this morning,
as if you singed my forehead
and then
healed it over.
Glow orange this morning,
wind.
I would like to feel your long wire
arms
slash
my back.

140

Fan this morning S
black jewel, be
pleasure.
Float under clear rippling
morning.
Magic letter S
Half-infinity.
Yin.
Contour.
S—

My image
—as I lean over to see you
... our aquiline
faces
touch
in the figure eight. Yes.
I lay you slowly on
to your side.

                                                        1973

ON A SHORE IN SERENGETY

          Hello
          O
black wild face
—of stalking cats
shimmering in the Savannah's
mid-day heat.
Ancient black face—
carved, and jewelled
a thousand years.
Hello,
fingers which have no joints:
purple leaves
are born beneath your nails,
and white lacteous grass,
spiders, a million

undulations.
Animals
                    —flee across your face
            hide,
or remain
still

—quivering—

...ready.

                I
circle
        circle
to seize your eyes
on a shore in Serengety,
where all animals recline.

1973

MY CLOSED ROSE FACE

Sweetheart, sugar plum baby, why in hell did you let me let you
leave me sweetheart, sweet plum?
Our house is draped dark and smudged in spider web.
The kitchen floor is littered with poison stumped
tree of heaven, and orange peels of our plan.
Backyard, a mango swamp and a desert are both growing.
Vines of cracked glass creep over the window.
Other's hands are touching me, kneading
my body into contortions of Not-You.
A white witch is beginning to understand me; she wants to settle
down.
Dog Sam licks her cheeks, and our black cat climbs her back.
She lies knowingly on our once bed of sky-blue sky.
Why did you leave me swimming in sand dunes of 'Truth', and
not
throw even one flower from our many rose-bushes in the front
yard?
In the paddocks of my calloused skin, white dismounted mares

ride away in an angry herd.
My stomach drops out every 100 yards I saunter down the street;
I've left stomachs abandoned on airplane seats,
in warehouse lofts, on small farms, and at your feet—
a stomach here and a stomach there.
A gaping drain has opened where the eye of hope whirled.

The mouth of a small blonde is perched like a bee on a bud
slowing munching me into her presence.
My thighs tremble to her taste.
She predicts the pouring of our marrow into a dog food can,
and cut your locks from the guitar so I can't
sing the gypsy return of your maroon lips.

Baby, why didn't you protect me from this supper
of myself playing all settings and the meal too,
when you could feel my body desperate for action
draining into their cups of grey?
Why didn't you cut your high cheek beauty open for my veins,
and rain on the closed rose of my face?
What is this faith of yours?

1973

SWEETHEART WITH NO NAME

Sweetheart with no name,
of myself, but not possessed:
(as air belongs to breathing)

>She
>like black damp
>through walls,
>transforms my mind
>to a touching sense

I swim in her salt white belly:
yet nakedness is too closed
for the touch I wish to make

Skin me

       she whispered

    you are Tiresias:
    I am your body.

1970

LOVE POEM TO A LESBIAN PROSTITUTE ADDICT

At night, men slip through your sweating flesh,
skating over wet sheets on which you entertain
their aching skin tucked
in moist lips, teeth, thorns, broken glass.

Each afternoon, cockless women don siphons for the visit,
eat you but cannot hold you in their perfumed cheeks.

Your tongue
flicks only their flake rouge—
all worship your criminal body
which will not come in a hundred ways.
                          Only
               the pure kiss
                the self-kiss
                  the kick-back
              mirror
        of a glass cock needle
           injecting your soft belly
        ...waiting...
                  for the cream hit!

                  the pure fuck
                  everytime
                  everytime:
and no chances.

1970

PUSHING

Into one pocket to
another, a white ball
popping: phoning one
after another a bookie
backing losers; laying
one after another, a wasp
spiking: each meeting pounds
against the bathroom
mirror like some fighter's face—
strung out on his own reel,
spinning, spinning out...

Hair an inch longer, a new tie,
a new tan—out
pushing again, overpowering
with the threat
of 'what you're missing'; with the challenge
of needing, which he feigns—
easing the way to becoming
cocaine; until you succumb
to his weakness, to his need, to his
threat; until you're strung out;
until you turn tricks
for his bag—which he sells
occasionally, which he
withholds.

1970

DINING WITH A FRIEND

My friend and I dined on his life
last night. We ate
until his bones became hangers
from which shirts of skin hung.
Mouthful by mouthful,
piece by piece,

eyeing his wife eyeing me, he reached
in to tighten his belt.
'Do you believe in God,
or yourself?' I answered Yes—
licking his wife inch by inch,
slipping her tongue until
she soaked entirely in my mouth.

Then he began to count karma coins,
piece by silver piece: the debts
would pay for eating, for causing—
he offered me 'more wine
young friend?' Listen

I'll throw water down, pernod,
even his best wine—Debt
is my own perception: Cause, my own
recognition! ...Anyway

I can always refuse to see.
I can always die. I can always
go back from where I came.

Come on honey! ...he's counting on our heat
to finish the job.

1971

ON WHETHER TO SIGN

Let me begin with a game—
a word game, and a mirror, a clock
and a mask. Also, skin—
(lumps of skin; or rather,
folds); and ...I need
desire.

Suppose you have only
(say) seven packs of time

to start with...
suppose I could double
that and throw in a new skin.
Would you be interested?

...Suppose I could stretch
one of those packs with a mirror
—make it feel like two, or maybe like three—
wouldn't you be *very* interested?

Look... you can't fight the world right?
What are you working for right?
If not now, never right?...
OK. At the top, I mean, when you're really high—
where the action is. Power.
I'm talking about power...
when you're *there*, a pack
goes a'hell of a long way.
Time is money Buddy, right? Money time.
Figure it this way.

If you waste your time,
you'll have to work for more right?
But if you don't count it, you don't spend it. Right?
If you don't spend, you save time—
then you can spend it all-at-once!
or even sell it a bit
to make ends meet...

Now I've got a connection, you see,
who makes things simple...I mean
you just owe him and no one else.
Things straighten out. Things get simple.
And it guaranteed
    to give you perspective.
       to give you incentive.

Suppose I could guarantee you (say)
Ecstasy, Immortality, and Fame—
you'd be interested, *wouldn't* you...Just
buy this.

Let me know if you like it; let me know
if you don't feel like a new man...
and there's *more* Buddy, plenty more
where that came from ...Just sign here.

1972

ELEGY

My friend is dead.
Suicide.
Snap. Gone. Just like that.
I wish I could do something:
pray? But neither of us believed. Or
write his divorced wife: no girl
was good enough anymore.

It was his choice.
I couldn't deny him that.
He wasn't an animal.
He wrote strongly
of men triumphing over life.

He kept telling me
at parties—'I'm no dog,
Allen. I'm no
dog.'

1971

THE GIPSY LADY ON THE CREAM WHITE MARE
(for John Berrvman)

'...And when I feel, fair creature of an hour,
    That I shall never look upon thee more,
Never have relish in the faiery power
    Of unreflecting love;-then on the shore
Of the wide world I stand alone, and think
Till love and fame to nothingness do sink.'
                John Keats

Upon a mare of cream white she rides.
thin pencilled eyes, and unbound hair,
    clatter of hands,
    hooves, rhythm of laughing
    flashing up!

...looking back, astride,
no other reins but light.

Clock-skin, mirror for the ride:
a dance of jewelled wind,
satin blood the texture of flame—
past sidewalks of grey carpet, alphabet trees,
bouquets of flowered eyes
and years

...running race which can't be lost,
like a mirror which itself
cannot see—upon thee John
she truly wailed and rode!
    Now drowned,
with the others... your eyes stream
past me—

Did you leap to join her?
weary of her maddening bolts:
one jump off the bridge, and your mind

complete.
Or having poemed your life, did you fear
you had lost her sight?
Did you refuse to walk
the remainder blind?

1972

DROUGHT 1972-73

I

On my property, as if within a lair, within fences,
I live behind gates, .303s, .22s, dogs;
under sheets of tin roofing
with etiolated grass, roaches,
red-backs springing to life.
Moths bang the louvers
like dust trout, their pink silicon eyes
shining and eager;
tea tree and wattle move down the clear
like a live relentless fence—
or a trail of ants.

The nearest town slouches over dry monotonous days,
dust winds grazing the main street, flapping
tin roofs like the laugh we had
about no rain.
Sometimes a thunder storm nears the mountain
—the sun twists through it like a red shoot
until it shatters.
Even animals seem fools
passing through their rain patterns:
birds swarming, huntsman spiders
entering the house in pairs.
Heat in an empty glaring sky,
in clouds skimmed to thinly from earth.
Leaves fall without gaiety.
Pools drop to their barest form.

150

Creeks jag and fall open dry.

Drought is a woman growing terribly old in the lane:
granite surviving, frail luxuries dead,
her skin stretching, and cracked like old leather.
We clasp each other slowly. I sweat
and turn away, our fingers still touching.

II
I intercede
and try to bargain.
Only certain things are said out loud,
and others not; certain things are done
and others not.
I speak personally to this drought:
walk round a fire;
wring linen on the garden.

III
Daytime it's hard
not to sleep.
I lie down in darkness
under bright tin roofing.
I lie and bake, through
drought sleep, day sleep,
..melting under hard sun.
 Drops
dripping from my forehead
gather me
in rivulets and creeks.
    Sleep,
washing through me,
    quickening,
in deepening streams
black deep gullies, in
black deep caverns
in caves
..white lacteous sleep.

A sleep
like the beginning
of hibernation.

1973

WHAT ANSWER CAN I GIVE

Susan is scrubbing factory oil from
my loft, her hair tucked in a cowboy hat,
her body in an apron of bright plastic;
my kittens at eight weeks
know the secret of life; my bird sings to his cage
above cats engrossed; the wastebasket
is stuffed with strawberry wood, and draft poems
from nights' past writing—

kindly my father has asked:

What are you doing,
wasting your life?
How can I answer?
What drove me here, on to the top flight?
Five years in flight
to this factory where they line
prams up my stairs, one after another,
wrapped in sheets and sheets
of brown, plain paper
like cheap dolls and mummies are wrapped; like
fingers pointing to a few years from now—
like my hopes are wrapped.

1971

AT TATHRA ON THE FAR SOUTH COAST

The salt air dripped small drops—
without moisture pitting the sand
beneath an abandoned flesh warehouse
through which

I used to fish: dreams for bait—
or a black squashed crab—hooked
to an invisible line in waves between the breaths
in their fight against the rocks

      the brass rocks which shone like walls
      splashed by passerby
      who hoped to dash
      brick into alleys and streams.

I picked glass from the sand and my hair
as the sun tired, and rolled
into a tin-foil sunset
which I carried to my room,
trapping the last of the earth in a shade
I was about to draw.

I extinguished even the stars
with my thumb, tracing a galaxy spiral
round the center in which I sat
dangling conceptions of my self
like bracelets.

   Again, next morning on the bay,
sparkling carpets headed for shore—
jewelled clouds poured rorschachs,
and the foam sparked!

I laid my self on a bed of crystals
in the shape of a knowing smile:
and advertisement for the one reputation—

a stone
splashing
in a tidal pool.

1971

LETTER TO MYSELF DISAPPEARING

As I disappear I become 'ruthless', and
as I disappear I become unloved—
without the possibility, as glass
cannot be loved.

As I disappear I become an object
to be tested, and fingers slip
off the glass of my skin—
then into a shrug of indifference,
and awe.

As I disappear I am questioned and accused,
walked around and given distance; and only
gladiators try me, no lovers.

As I disappear I have 'no enduring emotions',
no handles—I cannot be ridden,
or caressed; as I disappear

I have only this blank paper
to receive me, my hollow shouts,
my phantom needing; and soon, even it
will remain itself.

As I disappear I am being peeled and diminished,
like a slide stripping mountain, or a stream
carving a canyon—my flesh is being eaten away,
and I can't stop it.
...this red-yellow-orange ebbing flowing river
eating me away.

1971

KIKUYU GRASS

The trees can destroy you
for only so long,
the river can wash you away
for only a time;
you can lay in the field
and become the wind,
ideas can pass through your head
in gusts; but always

the kikuyu grass
pulls you down, ties you up,
folds you in diapers and blankets;

and you can be anywhere at all—
take a thousand walks over the hill,
but there's no way

when your body starts calling.
She calls you
back down.

                                                    1971

CITY NIGHT'S SWEET SHADOW

1
Night lowers herself
on squat haunches,
rubbing streets with shadow,
her children in bars and waiting parks
      'Quickly!
      before lights shut
      off! (killers and victims)

      Quickly!
      before all exits
      are sealed!'

...their teeth sparking:
light nippled fingers
beating flesh time,
chanting

    Old blood turns
    to water, water
    turns to oil

    New blood clots on
    blotters, new blood
    crusts in the sun

    Dim orange is
    powdered rouge—
    old alley hag!

2
Below the window's edge
—the voyeur
face awash in night
striped suit and tie yanked loose
moves like a finger slipping through silk
sees his face in bedroom mirrors
cleared and primal
freed from light; excited
by the coming true of pornography
he desires more than flesh.

And he's
right.
The moon is always for sale;
stars can always be
switched on: off

        Her mystery
      is always for sale,
      or can be lured into darkened

156

rooms with single beds, while
ads through yellow shades
flash into ears
filled with hot tongues and radio—

'baby..baby...'

To that tune
ecstasies are wrapped and sold.
Needle marks etch arms:
black backs stoop stairs,
thousands hang out
tapping
tapping

In boarded rooms
old men count toilets flushing,
creak open doors to each stepping:
rancid bodies
smeared on sheets of wine red—
faces flaking
off holes of O.D. dead.

3
Night, sweet city!

Sweet shadow
of forests and caves,
of fire and insects,
of attack and breath.

You are our only freedom: to buy
our own skin-death.

Shine your black flesh dress.

Ride the spotted black mare.

1970

HERE FACE TO THE FACE

God's inner body is the black universe.
She has punctured Her skin with stars
   for each child slain.

God's eyes are the Sun and Moon.
Her teeth are bare, desert mountains.
Her tongue is dry salt blue—
Line divides Her face.

God's voice is wind in the cypress trees.
   Waves, and this stream are the same.
Her Sun-eye winks at those lilac peaks
   overcome in the shadow of years.

Here let God appear to me at sunset
   like three stars:
Let me reach the red sky's moist fruit!
Let me dwell ecstatic in the Valley's
   green blossom:
Let me taste the white Wall's old bread!

I escaped the first century and the Russian
   nineteenth...
Like an old Jew, let me dance on my grave!

                                1972

THE SUN IS VISIBLE

'By the pyramid of sun you may draw a line.'
—can anyone explain the meaning of this, given in a dream?

I know that a ray of sunlight
is buried beneath the first pillar on the left
in the Great Mosque of Cordova.
 I can imagine this: a low
yellow light hard like a window bar.
Dante Alighieri gazed at the sun's face—

158

'I saw him sparkle... like iron from the furnace
drawn white hot.'

I wish to know
why I am irreversibly drawn into light.
A primordial duty, does it compel me?

★

    The sun is visible;
    my ornaments are gold;
    the rainbow my pleasure.

    I have seen a black crow turned silver;
    I have lain in the sand outstretched,
    and yielded.

    The eclipse of the sun is the clearest sign;
    and to die as fire, complete.

1973

VOICE

'I am lighter:
in front of strangers I sing.'
Also, it is their test.
Isn't everyone and thing a pretext?

    What is it about the rose, *exactly*?
    What is it about you...

I have sat wooden upon anonymous knees
talking, and talking:

A frail thin voice remains
of days and days new breaking.

★

To hold to that arching
which escapes my singing!
I also listen.

People are sometimes moved.
I am left behind.

You told me
cleanse yourself.
Rub against the rocks.

My face is shorn back against the wind
like a boy bike-rider.

1973

OPEN ROAD

Around valleys
of mood,
mountains rise:

each logic
makes its own sense.

The guidance
of predilection
or touch—

these two reeds
swirl in dream.

Freedom to follow it out:
this spiral spinning back
on to itself upon the point
of toy chance—

this open road
of determined joy.

1973

160

SAMOAN SONG

Mother, to live within you
not in mere earth but within breath,
within your breast cleavage,
in that damp salt taste.

To inhale your brown moist skin:
to fill my mouth with flesh—
your yielding, clay flesh.
To breathe time in slow dense waves,
back and forth rolling out like mats,
in melodious white lines:
To glide on to time.

To melt in coral-white sand, to age
like reef in effortless sun, under
relentless sun, drifting like a twig, twirling in dance.

    Mother, swirl me in your milk-white belly,
cradle me in the blood of your coated trunk,
I am eternally unborn: do not name me here—
do not name exile.
Press your belly in,
press me closer.

1971

THE BONE OF ONE FINGER

Of that loam, the parched rock within:
the bone of one finger remains Mexico,
whose adobe walls flake breaking paint, whose rot
wets every stone but survival.

Of the pyramids remain red ants
piling at their sites
monuments to power—but incidentally:
the streets teem with soft gourd shapes

and still proud faces, though
no one bothers with resemblance;
there is no pretension—
the squat giants are truly dead.
Their eyes have folded.

Even to a coward, not one potent lie
makes tempting an Aztec mask: the power
of his enemy's flayed skin
is worn in chapel splendour, its value
set by auction.

Like a brittle clay pot the old sun
cracked, fell to pieces
and was quickly buried; for what remains
a charge is made—
those grey brute mounds
of reconstructed stone and pastel lights,
those few smudges on dank-interior tombs.

The new sun rose; it shone
like a carnival in every village:
it bowed the people
handkerchief upon handkerchief,
to their knees before Guadalupe—in hand,
their children clinging.

They can tell you nothing
of pagan indians and their jewelled skulls:
under that sun of cold stone they do not lie.
There is no pretension.

1971

AFTER VISITING DACHAU

Every cream brick building;
                              every stack with black smoke
                              frightens me.
Every grey gravel yard.
                    Every cement shower.
Every park hiding buildings.
                         My eyes narrow.
My nose hooks hideously.
                        My beard grows shabby.
I stoop.
            My pockets fill with money.
Every uniform.
                    Every insignia.
Signs with stenciled instructions;
                              and every building
                              without windows.

Every dossier.
          Every census.
My face coagulates.
                 My skull bares.
Holes appear in my hands.

                    I can name no children.
                                             1972

CLASS OF '65

1
It was a time at Harvard in '62 when mushrooms
Were about to break the concrete ceiling,
When walls receded everywhere but in freezers and Berlin,
When negroes sought themselves personally, not speaking
Pure black to passersby; living quietly down South
Being tokens—a few others lived in a jail-like mosque.

In Cambridge, land of our forefathers (not mine),

Clean white shirts were improper and nouveau;
I produced frayed cuffs with sandpaper, wore holey
Shoes and striped ties; and primed for Sullivan &
Cromwell if they'd have me.

We were all special (even elite)
Each of us was a Potential
Each of us could make it Really Big
And I was proud.

My parents were proud
My fraternity was proud—
Who wasn't proud in those days'?

One night we watched ourselves stand up for America.
I couldn't back down, nor would they or the Cubans.
I can tell you we watched ourselves carefully—
We looked at the hard carpet, at our soft hands,
Out the glass windows

Feeling childish, meek—victims
In his, and in their, and in its hands: just
Beginning to realize.

2
It was a time in '63, when the Chinese
Made the grade alone, when Vietnam was first
Presented each evening for dinner; when the underground
Was built on newspapers and rubbish;
I chose between Tax, Corporate and Labor Laws.

I began to walk the Charles along browning
Banks, in ice, fog, deep blue introspection,
Deciding, if God existed, to take Labor over Corporate Law.
Everyday I walked in the freshening Cambridge wind,
Giving up lectures for walks...
I threw my Tax book out a four-storey window, and bought
It back shamefaced when Finals began:

I was as fragile as an autumn leaf blown—
Neither here nor there, neither this nor that,
Neither one nor the other...

One afternoon we sat silent watching Johnson
Swear in on an escaping plane;
We left for lectures knowing none would be held,
As did a hundred others gathered for the same reason;
I can tell you we looked hard.
We watched the ivy clinging to America cracking up,
The hate swelling seams, the plots thickening...

3
It was the time in '64 when Vietnam lay still
On no maps, when Watts sulked in the City Of Angels.
Before the Beatles climbed the string cross:

It was my last chance to meet the right girl,
To reap her reward and mine: I sought and failed everyone
But a black anti-semite (I owned no grocery store).

We loved each other.
I blamed her and she blamed me.
I learned what it was like when you can never hide,
The taste of black musk. She tasted kosher white.
By the time they crept into our bed, it was too late
To kick me out.

And the election was instructive that year,
We voted for Non-Escalation, Non-Defoliation, Non-
Involvement, Responsibility;
Voted against Goldwater, Them, a Minuteman army.
I can tell you that year we studied hard.

1971

165

THE INSTRUCTION

Des Leben lehret jedern, was er seir

                —Goethe

Life is teaching me by extortion
what I should be,
Rilke's solitude is not a mask
I can wear upon my entire face.
A laurel of time was placed on his shoulders
for each turning away.
The skin of his face shone, and was veiled.
I must continually give away, give away.
When I die they will cement the wall.
I may spend a few moments with some marvelous Nadja,
and a few men who'll imagine their lives, who'll
wait in the park to be recognized:
perhaps in that solitude, of
single molecules being shaped into light.

                                     1972

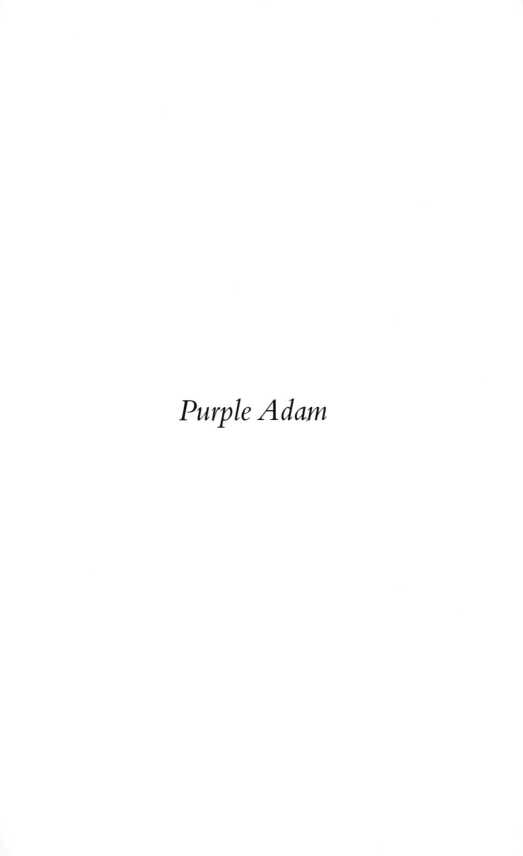

Purple Adam

I
PRELUDE

I can see mist smoking from the forested hills
around the farm—
I noticed for the first time today the white-eared honey-eater—
I see my new-born boy's astonishment, my wife's
beauty and depth;
I listen to the grunts of the doberman stretched
Near the fire, to the king parrots
in the orchard—
yet I live here near Van Dieman's Land
and somewhere near Poland.
I circle and circle above the house
like the wedge-tailed eagles—
I try to hold some truth which will not dissolve
in its own details;
Some virtue which will not twist into its own lie.

NARCISSUS NEAR BIRKENAU

Upon the virulent grass I spread a red tablecloth,
in this place trees boom, weeds burst into flower—
I place the knife and fork formally,
fill the cup with bright red wine.
The plates reflect my face.
Scattered around here is my people.
Scattered here is my ancient face—
through the caked maroon crust
I dig with cupped hands,
dig until
my lips kiss a skull.

A PLACE WHERE THEY REMEMBER

I watch my people, they cluster
at shop windows.
I am thinking of things to buy you,
things good to eat…old churches still stand here,
there are stalls of summer flowers, cafes with umbrellas,
smart, serious girls passing by…
Sun is glaring through the haze,
the sky a luminous field of gravel.
In this medieval square they haven't forgotten.
Children sense something.
A bugler calls from the dark-stoned St. Mary's.
I stare over my glass of tea like the others…
they whisper well—their lips vibrate, hum;
expressions smoothly retract.
Somebody has stepped out of line and has been dealt with.
Someone has been overheard.
A band of gypsies is shuffling among our tables,
Playing half-tunes, quick fragments. No one listens.
No one tips. No one looks up.

Cracow, 1977

COVENANT

Son, half-gentile child
I circumcised you—forced you. I made you bleed.
The *mohel* uttered words
I neither understood nor believed.
That primitive hour with sweet wine we toasted.
I was afraid to love you,
afraid you would turn against me—
your heart gentile, impregnable. The son created,
we entered the ancient covenant of fathers,
not to leave your body perfect.

MORNING NOON AND NIGHT

Months pass, Hungary pumps like an artery *judenfrei.*
Eden has put the proposal to the Secretary of Air:
the Jews are being deported, the Nazis defeated,
in retreat (this is 1944)—
when will they bomb the camps and its railways?
Each week the B.B.C. broadcasts atrocities,
a half-million lives are at stake. Months pass…
the wretches look to the sky each night:
the commandants plan their escape—
intelligence flows in—timetables, targets, detailed plans
(pilots volunteer) each morning noon and night
in a frenzy of a last meal, the ovens are gorged.
A prayer drifts over the camps—
Stalin Churchill Roosevelt

NGORONGORO CRATER

In the temperate highlands of East Africa
close to the Olduvai finds, some have likened Ngorongoro
to paradise: there zebras graze a vast grassland
watered by sweet springs, in the marshes pink-eyed hippos rise
and submerge—elephants browse under stately yellow fever
trees—
baboons trail along the crater's unbroken rim.
Soaring above the immaculate plain are birds of great stature;
the soda sparkles like Sinai. At daybreak,
predators methodically kill the helpless and young
survivors blink, drop their eyes. One by one
spotted hyenas rise from the mounds…
Serenity and indifference drift across the crater
like haze—

Tanzania, 1976

170

THE DISCOVERY OF THE NEW WORLD

They rub their eyes.
Come closer to the shore. Wait. Look.
Run to tell the others, they come.
They look too…a red pool widens;
the bush grows silent

SPRING SONG

Birds whistle. The birds are whistling
spring spring. Spring has come
Cloud sun. The clouds are all sunny
The fuchsia is out on top
bird whistle. The birds are whistling
dance. Everything is dancing
(You run like a bird—a brave man,
you very man—my very man
Spring spring. Because it's springtime
(dance, heel, toe behind, foot)

VAN DIEMAN'S LAND

In this land vague malevolence
hung upon the skin, olive grey, a gas…
Evil in the lungs, humming in the nostrils, flies;
world no one wanted to live in, an open pit—
sadism was twisted into the root
and snuff for floggin's—rum for amnesia,
boys for the laddies. *Fleisch und Blot.*
Eucalyptus too hard to cut, nothing sharper than a shell,
no animal of service, one edible fern, one fungus—
land without a fruit-bearing tree,
as though truth were exiled and the lie remained.
Here women would carry on their teats
small black skulls. Last of her race, the betrayed Eve—
Truganini, would die in a boarding-house.
This old, bloodied island, with their dark shadows

swept off the shore and the movement
in the bush—there is the smell of Poland
despite the sea breeze and the sheep dung.
Parklands root in mass graves,
the bush is a derelict house...Farmland is lush—
Flushed, deep, dark, maroon.
You who dreamed of an Australia
del Espiritu Santo, of the Holy Spirit—
this was the South, which is reversed;
the lost, fallen continent...
Weep for those who wandered through their garden,
who conceived with terror in their hearts,
for those we tore to pieces

REGENERATION
(Meeting at the Tasmanian Aboriginal Information Service, 1975)

Your face, Lorraine...
did you crawl on your knees and find it hidden
in that olive sea cave near Settlement Point?
Was it thrown down in the sand near some midden
screaming? Your race has been killed,
its features scattered without memory
(a flat nose here, black eyes set deeply there...)
I thought this face was forever exiled
in a wilderness of white semen.
You walk the streets of Hobart Town
and people don't rush for old shotguns—
you sit at that metal desk
explaining the current welfare schemes
correct, smiling at me
through your death mask.

AT WYBALENNA

Here a mute paddock, grazing merino sheep,
the planned graveyard, the brick chapel they've restored;
rubble outcrops and irises growing wild—
in this glaring winter sun. I walk to the long beach
over dunes, pick up sponges and cuttle-shells,
I walk back. Pick up a thumb-imprinted brick,
press in my thumb—and let it drop;
sit down on the grass and then I get up. Walk around
drink something fragments of tunes run through my mind.
I watch the vague outline of the mainland across the strait
sigh have something to eat stand around
at last a hard cough—my head is burning...
I lie down easily in your arms.

*Wybalenna: Site of the last Tasmanian Reservation on Flinders
Island

ALTAR

By thousands pilgrims' candles crowd in black metal carts
twist, melt, lean one into the other;
broken, flickering grotesque laughter—
the mongoloids, the palsied, shrouded, bent women,
grey cancerous faces, mothers encouraging middle-aged idiot
daughters, functionaries scurrying children's trolleys,
international banks, the massive trinket bazaar,
day after day, night after night, marches by torch-light.
We cannot bear this: sin offerings, guilt offerings
in every language. Hail. Each night is white with longing—
In the baths of Lourdes, in dimmed Sanctuaries,
incensed chapels—blankets and straps are removed,
pink nightgowns, striped hospital pyjamas—
below an arch of crutches
each mutilated body; man's kept-secret in rooms,
committed in institutions body. Oh, children
your pitiful bodies—each man his own body
is offered in the Temple,
in a monstrous pieta—   Lourdes, 1977

THE CEREMONY FOR MR. NADJEK

A certain Pole, a short bespectacled bureaucrat,
once a friend of Meir, flown into Jerusalem,
now stands at attention...the cantor is singing,
the rabbi prays, the administrators speak in his honour.
From Borislav he supported the world:
night and day he refused to be dishonored—
two years he lived beyond human nature.
Day by day, in his attic, in caves, in drains
he saved the Meirs...he fills the hole with vigour.
Rising, he says something in Polish which attracts laughter;
then, *L'Chaim!*
As the group leaves the Memorial Room
I break through, trying to touch his arm—

Jerusalem, 1976

PIETA

I leave it for you to say why it is
that every moment we are awake we do not weep?
How is it we walk the streets
and do not fall on our knees before anyone
who is still beautiful, or who is ugly?
I think of those pyramids in sealed chambers;
of those crazed in ghettos
who ate the arms of their children, frozen in urine.
Would you picture this with me?
How is it we are able to forget them;
that we dare to have other than those children?
I think of the mute, black children
their mothers held by the scruff of the neck
for the minutes it took...why is it
we do not memorize each name, every word whispered,
the texture of the ground, the color if the clouds,
the killer's gestures...
Why is it that every moment we are awake we do not weep?

INVENTORY OF TWO GRASS BAGS DROPPED BY
TASMANIAN WOMEN, NOW IN THE LAUNCESTON
MUSEUM

1.
Pieces of red ochre
wrapped in animal skin—
A few scraps of glass obtained from a settler—
An echidna quill—A few berries—

2.
Lumps of black greasy material—
Several pieces of tool-making stone—
Two feet of an infant—

THE REAL IS NOT ENOUGH

No one is here.
Not even at the gate.
Squinting, I keep going, mind reeling…
Liebe Mutter! If my eyes were seeing these buildings,
if they were seeing this place then.
As far as the eye can see—fences, towers, barracks in glare.
Hot grey haze, vast—hopeless—my head lowers.
 A narrow mud path mown from one barrack
to the next—I walk up, down. Hour upon hour
…the women's section, the families' section, the gypsies' section
float in weeds. Trains hoot, shunt: a railroad track leads straight
to a mass of rubble…Somewhere a group is laughing,
they are shouting a girl's name— A family passes,
they read a guide-book out loud, like a lecture—
Every word carries like a shot—
I want to scream: are you crazy?
I rip out a handful of flowering weeds.
…anyhow, I've seen enough.
I won't be the keeper of this place.
Teenagers are scrambling up a guard tower—
Someone is translating the crematorium sign—

I break a strand of rusted barbed wire,
hide it in my sleeve. In my pocket, dried rotten straw
from a bunk in the women's section.
Others are coming, a group is leaving their bus…
I walk out with no thoughts, feet burning
along the main camp road—
What is the truth which fills the mind with light?

Birkenau, 1977

II

LETTER TO AN UNBORN CHILD

Things have made themselves ready.
Our life flourishes. We have found this place.
You were conceived in love.
Hurry, complete yourself…
Listen child, I am waiting for you.
Your father is waiting.

PURPLE ADAM

Purple Adam is twisting as we're laughing,
that's the girl—PUSH—he is writhing,
the umbilical cord coiling his neck
—he's out! into matter-of-fact hands.
We were not convinced, even that long night,
that God's eye witnessed our life.
We strive through endlessly discovered worlds—
wear out, die…
Blind life propagates blind life.
Only, through the infant time was made
visible—suddenly judging us, running out…
this terminal slap became the vortex of
our abandoned aspirations; suddenly reborn to us—
our secret hopes.
Blind as sperm we conceived our own witness.

176

NOT READY

Each day searching begins:
eggs and morning tea, yes—
but not a lover (unless in her actual arms,
unless his eyes gaze into her actual face).
Days crackle like lizard skin. Things disperse—flee
through chromatic bush
(or there's a slight streak, a jerk.
A flapping somewhere for a second.)
Memories slither into dark, empty holes
of experience. He won't believe in people's
brisk determined walks through downtown Sydney;
he's not ready to embrace emptiness
From one bookshop, around one side of the harbour
he walks to the other—filling in time between meals.
To every wisdom, against every razor,
he turns, and is returned—
thinking of himself as a word
which must contain a hard-core meaning

WORKING LAND

Now I've moved on to land, I'll work it.
The '71 flood ripped its stomach out.
Entrails and sinews dry on sand and granite.
Creeks wind like blood trickling
in shattered limbs.
Gradually, oil soaks through the skin of gums
whose heart is eaten and burst.
Marrow is gnawed in every log lifted.
Hundreds of charred ribs jut from the soil.
The dog brings a carcass of kangaroo
whose paper black skin is like a cocoon
dried tight...
I think how the doberman would skin, of where
his flesh is thickest. Do I cut around
the rear paw, cut upward
toward his hind legs and belly, then scrape out
the offal and coat; or work like a butcher and hack?   1972

REALITIES ON A MARGINAL FARM

Here the electricity is an abstraction,
and the cheques; but I butcher the animals,
the orchard shrivels in the fall,
the garden burrows and coarsens in winter.
The work is tangible—to kill the bush;
three seasons' stacks are burning.
What stands, I let stand for a purpose
(beauty is a purpose); the trees fall at my feet.
But the bush does not collaborate.
From a protracted city visit, anxious—the first glaance
tells me the land is alright. The second, it has indulged me…
that it will be a life's work to make this my garden;
that I will need two sons. Brute sons.

BROWN SNAKE BY THE FOWL-SHED

I blasted your arched, serene face—
I should have been willing to watch,
you made no movement to strike
content in the morning heat, watching as the shotgun arrived.
A blast slammed you high against the iron;
as I reloaded you disappeared.
You could have struck first easily—
two feet from my leg you remained content
to watch me back away

I WATCH MY SON WITH ASTONISHMENT

I watch you with astonishment. I love you so much
You seem so far then turn to me delighted
I cannot remember you from the day before
I am like a wounded animal. I close my eyes—
It is impossible to live this way.
On a special occasion I culled a young gander,
dropping it squirting blood from the neck
I look to the flock but they returned to their grain
If anything should happen to you
I will always call you, I will always be seeking you

THE PET JOEY

You stretch on the Bukhara rug in gold rays
of morning sunshine, a boy prince of sublime beauty and line;
you show me the reposed power of male beauty.
In the orchard you play like a strong youth
but in the bush you would be shot in the first spotlight—
Soon too powerful, a danger to the baby—
I want to let you go. Castrated or penned,
I must choose the method to destroy you.

THE JOEY'S DEATH

Still the joey's death rips my body open like his.
I cannot exorcise it, a small thing in its way.
I didn't feel this for the goslings I dragged from the coop
shitting in fear. And what's the use hitting cats
when you find wings torn off in the kitchen,
or a kitten rabbit's gnawed face? The cats are mine,
I have power over their life not their nature.
I thought to offer a hundred dollars for those dogs,
but in my hands now they'd await commands or food.
To shoot them I'd have to re-enact their kill.
I know the call the joey made is the same cried
for millions of years; that the power of those dogs,
their joy in it, is virility in life, maybe a form of play.
I would have done anything to protect you,
I could not act. I was not there.

THE MYXO RABBIT

In an outcrop of granite a rabbit crouched—
slowly disintegrating, it staggered blind
within feet of the garden gate—its brain churned to pus,
eyes shut like a boxer's in coma;
as if to judge me it displayed its face and waited.
My shot broke its neck;
hind legs in spasm, then long, even motions—

the second splattered the face. Earlier, the dog
had brought another; dark with saliva it crawled in circles.
In a high crook of a tree, its neck wrung, I placed
an offering; but this one blended into the fowl-shed mud
untouched for days. There are arguments of practicality
and economy. The mosquito injects the virus;
before the rabbit, four dairies milked here—
now twenty cattle can't graze.

A DIVINE VISITATION

I had just written
"Justice confuses us with its idea of symmetry"
in the book of history I was reading
when, backing down the stairs into the bedroom
—murmuring and gurgling, grunting and singing
appeared the child his grandparents call divine.
"Hello stinkpot..."
he turns and turns in a small circle... hands me
his mother's skirt from the floor;
flapping his arms, beaming—
he climbs, pulls, rips everything apart.

THIRD CAT

A black stray cat sitting on the road
stopped us at the top of Big Jack,
and refused to run.
Until the others could accept
this third cat, we kept her separate;
so thin, but clearly she had come from a home—
and been dumped.
Later we found yellow sprays of vomit from the milk;
the nobules of cancer on her back and neck.
Revulsion was like an electric shock.
I just dropped her.

Our compassion wasn't strong enough
to let her die in the house.
I packed her in a potato sack
—and nauseated, as if with wet carrion
I drove back to Big Jack—
instead of killing her.
In two weeks
she found a way down the mountain
and sat at the door,
calling.

1973

THE EXPULSION

Everything I say now ends with threat
—or I'll smack you or I'll put you to bed, do you hear?
Didn't you hear what I said?...
But he doesn't want to; or sit on the potty—
or enter the world of his daddy.
I force him, then lose conviction—
I want to join him, to live without discipline;
no how or why, in one song—
outside his daddy's world of right and wrong.
Then he wants to be serious, to be like me,
to be my equal—

THREE GENERATIONS ALONE IN THE HOUSE

This afternoon, instead of reading
I build Lego blocks with Adam's set.
In the bedroom sleeps my father
deteriorating beneath my hands,
failing despite my commands
(Dad, lift your leg—)
I try to draw his head out of fatigue,
out of resignation; but I think
he doesn't have anything to live for.
His face brightens around Adam
as it must have around me—

I jerk him into further humiliation
(Let the tablecloth go, Dad—)
Three generations alone in the house,
I treat my father as if he were myself.
Four-year-old Adam plays
with his only granddad,
and protects him from his son

MERIMBULA BEACH

These basalt boulders here in the sand,
up to their necks in fine gold sand—
as though elephants were buried
and the swash against their puffed cheeks
were white wasps and green ants—
Well the surf's up! Laughing—"Come on in."
Laughing—"Come on in, man, come on in, man."
(I wonder what it's got up its sleeve)
OK, here I come! (with a fin, man).
And all those people on vacation
here walking around cooling it in white sun;
and all those bulge-eyed black kids with enormous
doddering heads… All the obesity and blond hair
and teeth smiling, turning themselves over and over again.
All these birds here at Merimbula—
the occasional cormorant flapping across the surf line,
the seagulls cocking around, this beak quaking
in my ear Allen, death. Death, man—
Al-len, death—
Death, death—

SUMMER PICNIC IN COW BAIL CREEK

Electric the flies stings. Electric the dragon flies
Sheet-iron whiteness—ringing. Flash of copper wire
a startled lizard—electrocuted the trees—
charred wattles burned out—humming.
The yellow streaked wattle-bird—flitting.

182

Orange, lone butterfly flickering-flickering—
Tension. Cracked granite. Silent, dry storm.
Spent lightning—in dirt.
Puff-ball condensers, thistle condensers
humming. Scratches on the skin. Pricks.
Baby screetching. The cicada whine—
Face in glare. Coiled. The corner eye
flickering—th   th   th   th

CLEARING REGROWTH SCRUB

Early sun breaks through night's rain formations.
So many birds outside uncurtained windows
I can't read poems of Lo-T'ien. Regrowth scrub
scabs my shimmering light green paddock skin—
either I lower bedroom blinds or climb the hill
but I lie, a stone in bed. Adam making a great commotion
"playing quietly," my wife brings me eggs and tea.
I can lie this morning reading Lo-T'ien; my eyes close.
Taunting, the scrub cleared three years ago.
Reaching for the Heaven of Bliss Fulfilled,
regrowth must be uprooted—on the hill of Flux
or in the Mind of Fleeting Images
Hit! lever dogwood—chain saw, pile it.
Hill emerges—pasture is long and stubbly
around my mattock pocks; granite outcrops pick out sun.
I become ambitious, I should continue;
then lose heart, weeks in it…
I clear what I can see lying down from my window.

RIVER POEM

1
Now I rise, rise myself, the incarnate jewel flickers,
a sapphire spark—the back of my hand pulsing,
saliva sharpens in the glands, converging with
the amazement everywhere, with what is always here,
perpetually repeating; this morning—in the air

the new grey kitten leaping, in scarlet fuchsia
the white-eared-honey-eater...Adam's sheer physical beauty

2
Dragonfly flies by—white butterfly
jags a path like a window crack,
flies ricoshet off my repellent sprayed skin
tall manna leaves
tumble twirl
down slowly
upon my shoulders

3
I know I can't hold this oneness with the world;
world always here, certain. Mind was not meant to be natural,
to remain invulnerable, animal. The problems I push away
become my enemies' voices; pushed away, become philosophers'
...Being melded, I fissure; being embraced, I am ripped away.
I can't be free of what I think, mind fights me for its life—
A sword whirls in my mind; I can't be here, or in any other place.
Between banks, between minds, thought and thought,
voice and voice, flows the river: river,
river, always here.

4
These white skinned eucalypts
hair dripping as if risen from the river;
careening, tall, with their thin necks
and delicate collar bones—I spread my fingers
to the tips of their lowest branches.
Hard insect click ringing TZIT   th   th
Sun hovers on rim of the cliff my eyes throb.
The pool is gold, spirals as I enter...Eden water—
eyes thick, blurred; I tumble suspended in its shimmering sack.
Down river wind forms, ocean sounding—the girls feel it first,
they're jolted, it rocks them, wheels them; I rock in rapids of river
and blue-cresting bush. This morning I go down to the river;
voices drive me.

184

TONIGHT

My son made me laugh so hard tonight,
he was daddy, I was baby; my son made me cry so hard tonight
because I wanted my father to laugh like us tonight—
his son wanted to make him laugh like us tonight;
My son made me laugh so hard tonight,
I am afraid to close my eyes tonight
so he will be with me in the morning when I awake,
so he will not be me in the morning when I awake

I SING

The song is singing, I sing tari tari tari
I call you. The wound opens. I strain, reaching for the voice
I reach a strained, spiraling voice. I reach you
I reach you. I listen to you sing, old woman
I sing higher. Your son is singing, old woman
ai tari tari. Tari tari

HOMELAND

Sunlight slides down the hill towards the house, day begins.
My life slides gently, quickly by—A man from no specific country,
from a mass city; grandson of refugees, son of migrants
passed away. I dangle roots into this thin soil of a family
and rough farm. Here I change the landscape, I exist.
My son will not learn from me his grandmother's tzigane songs,
nor see with his father's alien eyes
but he may inherit his father's house, he may live
where he was born…but he will move quickly away,
into an anonymous mass

ASIA MINOR

Once the New World, Ephesus—
then gradually, a province of Empires,
growing yet more wealthy, life easy.
A renowned Temple, amphitheatre, rich brothels
(there were decent artists, sculptors,
a great philosopher); refuge for the exiled,
for expatriates, comfortable.
Once the New World, its broad processional way
lined with columns of colonial administrators;
I linger on ancient marble sweeping
between worn Turkish hills,
in a landscape where each rising step is a labour.
I feel I have lived here—
too distant to settle without resentment;
never intending to die here, arguing with myself,
participating with half-heart in its foreign,
secondary culture. In Asia Minor
on a remote estate withdrawn from public position,
in dialogue with my work—at times with the Masters'
or merging with the forest and its nature,
trying my hand at agriculture;
winters, in mute labour
when I should have left for Athens or Jerusalem—
time to time visiting bizarre ends of the Empire
self-exiled, in search if some ancient self—
or to annihilate the self—
freed of too much caring, drinking with benign strangers
left to raising my family, to purify a poetry

                                        Ephesus, 1977

A MAN'S REACH

After seeing the limestone pyramids of Gizeh
I didn't mock the vanity of Pharoah;
The wasted effort, the duplicity of the fellahin—
I felt a sympathy before their great monuments.
After seeing dolmens still balancing,

186

And stone-age huts in a farmyard like mine,
I realized that it was not beyond a man's reach.
In a year a bulldozer could build
What took hundreds of men years—
Something for the ordinary fact
I lived here.
Something that no one would bother to break up,
That would last as long as the earth
As real as Silbury hill.
If in his spare time, a man
Climbed to the mound and worked alone
He could build something permanent.

PASSAGE

I feel my face passing through the membrane
of having a father,
passing into the landscape nearer death
—in which my face replaces his face—
the landscape of what is
that surging, dreaming divers surface to;
from epicentres of my ego and my expectations—

Silbury Hill: a large man-made neolithic mound in England
Landscape in which I become strange to my wife, to those
friendly to me,
in which no witness lives who knew me as a child.
To myself, I become imaginary, my sole creator
I close my father's eyes, feeling my eyes
begin his gazing;
the membrane through which I pass
—the skin of my father, of the father dying first—
already drying; cataracted upon what they see,
and are bound to see, further, harder...
but not from passing from a happier time,
or from a child's garden, or from the possibility of a woman's love
I feel the son's realizations of the father
—for the first time, father—

passing from the son's domination,
from the son's experiencing
to the generation of the father, names revolving;
being which I do not yet know but praise because I taste it—
Landscape of the acceptance of the father's death,
of emerging into death,
in which my son-face replaces his face,
in which my eyes replace his eyes
in which my skin replaces his skin,
ahead of my barely conscious son

THE CREATION OF THE WORLD,
THE CREATION OF ADAM

The white-backed magpie twirls an early mystery song
and the olive brown snake the prototype of dance—
through yellow nights, the masked owls;
the goanna on his branch, silver days.
My blood is running free
my flesh returns red as clay—
head swaying in the west gale
my eyes explode in sun—
The bush sparkles silver—the sky is spirals—
Adam begins the world again!
I have new infant eyes, I have these new fingers

THESE FALL EVENINGS

These fall evenings are good.
I smell my own charcoal sweat, my mind glows
empty. Muscles hum gently.
Hard, mute physical work; clearing scrub,
mixing cement—jobs with no real hurry.
Now it's time for Adam—
I become a mountain, he is Hillary;
I am a crocodile, he's a plump bait—a ball bounces
around in the kitchen, blocks are built, and go crashing;
the fire is burning slowly… news

rambles in the background.
As I pull off my boots, he runs up with slippers;
carefully, backwards on my toes he hangs them.
O Adam these evenings are good.
Everything is worthwhile.

IF THERE IS A PARADISE ON EARTH…

I stroll the surface of my land;
mattock, dig, pick. Chain saw. Clean, rub it
—because it's mine and I want it to look good.
Bold, naked. Every contour expressed like oiled muscle.
Lying in the sandbox with Adam, we look
across the river onto malachite hills…
sharp shadows are cast across a quarter-mile.
Now, this is what I like. I can see every pore
on my arm, the granite outcrops jut like fiords,
the light is rich Jerusalem gold.
insects by the thousand sparkle.
My heart is singing—
It is here, it is here, it is here

JERUSALEM

Low cloud moving imperceptibly towards the sea
quiets the farm—
day suspended no different at dawn than sunset
horses' hooves don't quite touch ground
geese make no sound, the dog does not chase rabbits
Enclosed in natural cocoon,
in the embrace of the bush
in realization—
content to watch from inside luminous skin revolve around me
I feel my face turn; flesh thin as a wing
Dreaming chrysalis tumbles in the cycle of recurrence
Forced by the principle of spring
the ornate son will hurl himself and his sons
towards the gold fire-mouth

1980

EARLY MORNING AND A POEM OF KIM YUK

Early morning is creamy with mist
birds woke me up—
caws, cracks,
piping mixed with burbling down the sink,
sewing machine chirping,
tsees stitched together with ca-aaaws
My wife is writing down her dreams, we lie turned aside
bottoms touching;
the peacock walking on the water tank
makes a giant kettle drum boom
Be sure to invite me
when your good wine is brewed,
now he trumpets
ktreehaw, kee-ya;
now only caw-aw —aaaws
Sam shakes his ears by the window, jumps the fence
into rabbit paddocks—
they stop when he stops, old Sam—
white kitty plays with a rabbit's head
in the kitchen
I'm thinking of laying a pipe from the high dam
to make a shower;
yesterday we hiked to the waterfall—reclined, smoked
…and I'll invite you if blossoms
bloom in my garden;
the new baby has five weeks more in hospital;
we'll see what happens, what happens to our playing
we'll discuss, then, how to live
a hundred years without worry

Kim Yuk, a Korean poet of the 16th century.

TAKING POSSESSION

I plant myself in this earth
coming so late maybe I'll never belong
land which must become my paradise
I am not who I am
I don't start from the beginning
I know labour and what land can mean
but the things I do are very deep and strange
not themselves
not planting cypresses and fruit trees and olives

Clil, Israel

PASSING

Sweetness is in me
the land's humming in my body
coming out of the fields,
arms swinging loose
no strength to hold them.
I turn towards the cool red sun.
Rain has pleased the land—
blue erodium, chrysanthemum,
red and white anemone undulate
in the current of my passing through and the green wheat

THE OTHER SIDE

Moon descends the other side of the sky—
night deepening behind mountains that will flame
Rocks open weightless
larvae whose fatness splits their shells,
forms of black vegetation stiffen;
wide-eyed animals cry to each other
edged into wind caves, folding silver wings
Darkness sucks into wounds

LISTEN

Listen to the wound
where you separated
that alone knows you
and was promised you
from the start—
listen with the rawness
of a desperate animal
She is with you—
her violent whisper

THE BLUE THE VANDALS LEFT

The blue the vandals did not touch
is the blue that penetrates death,
deep violet blue—the blue that matters
they left the white saint's
or the idol's face they touched—the initials scratch at his eyes
his peculiarly sensitive, brown eyes

Church caves, Anatolia

GEMATRIA OF SIGHT

Glass (stilled) in rushing water:
water − skin = wind
sun + silence = glass
garden in clear desert = fire
is a place without death

IN WIND

My eyes of tiny mirrors
sparkling silicon flecks in wind
carrying brilliant mountains

In the Other

PREFACE

Thrown out on the shore—
you listen to the song
that was sea
black mountainous peaks
slow ancestor faces
break over the other
the desert is pulsing
in your throat
how the eagle aches to cry out

1
As you pass
flowers open to deadly sun
not seeing the spectacle
of themselves in the wadi,
or smelling the pungent perfume
as their leaves crush,
the lengthening light turns your eyes
towards them—
as you pass
seed spirals in the wind
Violet stars, red disks,
globes with yellow rays
break the iron *hammada*★
they bloom in your eyes
Their World to Come

★hammada : hard desert crust

194

2

Excitement in the air—
the birds' calling—
bird whistles
of ringing crystal
ring sing me
Swirling from your throat
out of limestone caves
everything that dies
soars over strings
over your fields of rhythm

3

I feel your flights—
your shoulders' power
the silhouette of a bird's face
inside a man's face
Birds who gyre
in violence
open and close in me
Fly in the sight of my eyes, eagles—
the flights of our desire
rise in the soar
of my uplifted face

4

O I am falling
towards you—
wheeling the sky
falling up
falling until I can't seem myself
until nothing will be left

5

Ibex make trails for you
down crumbling mountains
to the pool
for as long as the flowers
endure
the wadi climbs
water turns stone for you
Your head thrown back
hawks—
spark—
mica—
your lips
sip the mirror,
their faces spiral in

6

May I offer you
maroon and black rocks
this slice of Macintosh apple?
do you know what sweetness is
may I offer you
anything as tangible
as this place to sit in wind;
or may I only
leave you alone?
The canteen spills
you shine—
your maroon deepens

7

In silence
you see pleasure,
white magma pulsing
out of the beginning

8
Night,
shard light, shot into everything
the smell
of fresh
silence
the sound
of rushing water
falling
particles
raining
raining glass, shattering

9
Dawn.
a sun opens emptiness
a word pronounces over and over
A hot day glitters

10
Tulip
breaks the fissured crust
its wondrous red, black satin robe
from a hidden kingdom
in the powdery loess,
you kneel beside it
her cup of colors
invites your tongue
The next sight waits
refusing to wait
thousands of red satin drops
slopes papery pink and maroon with sun roses
the Negev's blood-drops drying

11
The flies' frenzy
in my face—
the whirl of my hands
slap my own face
criss-cross the flies' biting
I have to find wind—
driving me out into the sun—
I run towards the shadeless mountains

12
Wind in my ears
try to think
can't think
only the wind's power
lets me know wind
know pressure
screams in its pressure
calls, whistles fade shriek
My eyes colors gusting
in the wind's direction
breaking against my forehead
against my back
turning me
to fly—
hair a frenzy
to do it—
to give in—
slammed in the chest I am lifted
arms lifting
holding my breath
backwards stumbling back towards the cliff

13
—Full sun—
no cloud
no shadow
to hold onto
to open my eyes to
to burn in their oil
to return my calcium
and traces of mineral
my voice to its high ringing

14
Raven
the most evolved
of all birds
floats over heavily to have a look
at a man squashing apple into rock,
at a man talking fast to the sky
as if the sky were hunched over him
caws others to
have a look—
Empty shadows coast
across the boulder
slap
my face

15
Above. water on fire—
shivering in the pleasure of water
skin the pattern of wind-swept water
shoals surging in configurations of gematria
of poems read into water
as my hand thrusts fingers burst into sapphire
Oh I am happy, really happy—
nowhere to reach—
a figure in an eagle's flight
shatters the glass
crawls onto shore
bleeding gashes in his flesh
gasping

16
Chip me away
to the contour
of your hand
until I am right
to use—
Then don't throw me away
into the dirt
don't leave me here

17
In silence
I return to silence
to say yes
through I, the mirror
at its center
to hear yes

18
Now its heat is from a far away fire—
light withdrawing as the sun presses down
each bush and rock releases shadow
the last proof of physical reality
—a hare springs in skidding flight
to the sun-lit crater floor
Every stone has turned to watch
the eastern cliffs
each rock a half-moon
behind, the sun projecting—
I turning around and around,
feather and stipa grasses are alight—
strokes of silver and platinum
every seed pod and grass shines
Shadow surging over the saddle
swallows my legs
I can't run—
my hair light

19
On this peak—
this clear place
I can't stop
my heart
its crudeness:
the pump doesn't stop—
the hum of mind's egoism
doesn't stop—
It doesn't matter
what the truth is
I can never know—
It's my choice—
to say yes
The clearer the place
I can't stop
my heart
the loves surge through me
the more I believe my union

20
I climb—
don't bother to look around
until I recline in the ibex's soft lair
and close my eyes
in red darkness
the waves of breathing
quiet swells
orange, yellow currents
swirl in eddies of
reverie
ears dream, drifting past
sounds of meaning
into stillness that surrounds them
the high ringing from everywhere

21★
A man whose family
disappeared
into unsharable memory,

no one is left
who knows the
child

left with eyes on him
their names for him

      ...skating all the way up the block
        to answer his mother's calls

calls from a long time ago
to himself,

         Allenyu, Allinka

A man
disappearing into experience

taking his sons with him
is calling in himself,

hold onto me
Try to know me

22
Jiggling Yshai in the air—
with his watery blue eyes
and his old man's silky skin
is like bouncing my baby father in the air
Oh how he laughs in anticipation!
Oh how I'm going to throw him in the air and catch him!
He grins as he looks down at me—
he knows how much I miss him

★*There are several versions of this poem, others more personally speaking
with his sons. This version was put in the series*

23

I roll the pumpkin he rolls it back
it doesn't reach—
he crawls behind shoving with one hand
concentrating, puffing, sticking out his tongue
wobbles it over to where I'm hanging over the couch
I like the way he likes to play
roll the pumpkin
and shaking things then slamming them on the floor
as he looks at me over his shoulder—
and the way he likes me rubbing his tummy like a puppy
and the way he can laugh through such a tremendous amount
of tickling—
Yshai's ready
ready any time to make trouble—
he catches me watching
his eyes like glittering oil
and the way his play is a rushing stream
we are laughing so hard I don't know if it's crying—
shuddering so hard it becomes quiet
with terrible animal faces
a man suckles his son

24

The earth blistering, pink flesh peeling
furrows filling with eggs
just in time—
the wind shifting from the south—
rain catching my mouth,
rain like a crazy animal—
I can't hold my smile back!
teeth sinking into my shoulders—
jumping all over chasing the tractor to the house
First rain! the land laughing and having a good time
(later sun will light the outcrops' silver
and the streams of mercury, mirrors everywhere—
your eyes kings!) falling, drifting...
becoming meditation

long soaking breaths
I can't breathe without rain
the slow penetration inward
into a man's pregnancy

25
Land where I move trees around
and plant rooms of blue and green cypresses

listens for boots
for the tractor

land wanting to please
to be fertile
to be formal, liking cycles and rituals

The earth like night in my hands
not lifting my head from terracing darkness

enclosing fields, enclosing the hill
and the wadi—

in my heart I have died here

26
The space that even
we cannot cross to each other
that surrounds each of us
separates everything,
a mother feels first—
that her foetus doesn't belong to her
that the cord is attached
to a presence,
the space that is the stillness
each of us dies into
is our hope

27
She who used to pray
that I become a tzaddik,
now prays that we remain beautiful
in each others' eyes—
the wounds of our life will be healed
by dying together

28
You, who are the blemish—your beauty
is the war in reality fighting for perfection

29
Maybe I can sing tonight
in the quiet room
from the throat's wound
rise voices of man and old women,
melodies sung hundreds of times
so different from my life
or head back
a strained, transparent voice—
and the song
can arch for a moment in revelation, a scratch of light
The woman of my voice
who was lifted like a bride
from the white room—
maybe I can sing tonight
be sung by power,
a voice opening darkness
and I am her

30
Left is space
the place you were

our faces turned
back to back,

your white nakedness is my silhouette
against the night
you are my freedom
the boundary of everything else

From my cries
from the penetration of our kisses
from your luminous return to my body
is left space
the place you were

is my
aloneness
is endless

31
The smell clings to my skin
like a most beautiful woman's
who I have clung to
as she loosens the corona of her hair;
her taste under my tongue
and on my eyelids
between my fingernails

Our pleasure that is the eclipse of the sun

My friend, my deepest friend—
I bury my face in the brightness of your hair;
through your eyes my mind fills
with everything to hope for

My eyes are shimmering white animals
that you capture then set free
drained of colors;
they are like ibex who recline
under soft chalk ledges
watching for you

Still the crown pulses where
you entered into our uncompleted love—
I was flung open in utter darkness
until there is no end to our embrace

My face hides in you

SOME ANSWERS BY ALLEN AFTERMAN TO QUESTIONS BY YOSSI KLEIN HALEVI

Q: When you began writing, what vision did you have of yourself as a poet?
A: I was never interested in writing to heal myself, or watching my blood on the floor. I was attracted by an older idea of poetry. The poet has obligations—to know reality, to hold as much of the world as he can. I took that responsibility seriously. I came to be a poet out of strength.

Q: And that same sense of responsibility motivated you to become an identifying Jew?
A: Becoming a Jew was connected with becoming a poet. I started reading about the Holocaust. It was a deliberate decision: now that I'm going to be a poet, I have to face this thing. The more deeply I read, the more I realized I had to go to the camps. In 1976, my wife Susan and I spent a year in Europe. From there, we came to Jerusalem.

Q: Moving to Israel meant leaving a promising career as an Australian poet and becoming virtually anonymous. Wasn't that a hard transition?
A: In Australia I got a lot of recognition. But when we made aliyah, we just got into our lives here, building the farm. I didn't mail out a single poem in ten years. It seemed abstract. But all this time I never stopped writing. Over the years I developed the faith that if the work was good, somehow it would get out. My job was to write it, not to plug it.

Q: And now your second career has begun.
A: The day after I finished *Desire for White*, literally the next day, I got a call from Stanley Moss, whom I didn't even know. It was an amazing instance of *hashgacha* (providence).

Q: How did that happen?
A: Yehuda Amichai had mentioned me to Moss. I had a very tangential connection with Amichai: I'd once given him a copy of

Purple Adam. And now, years later, Stanley Moss calls out of nowhere. Can you imagine, sitting in Clil with zero connections, not having published in ten years, and you get a call from Stanley Moss? I gave him *Desire for White* with no hope what so ever. I mean, who's interested in religious poems? He read it and said, 'I'd love to publish it.' I said, 'Oh.' (*laughter*) Then he asked me if I had anything else. I said, 'Well, there's this manuscript called *Kabbalah and Consciousness.*' That was really pushing it, but I figured, what the heck, right? (*laughter*). In twelve hours he took both books, and brought them out in nine months.

Q: Besides not getting published for ten years, how did moving to Israel affect you as a poet?
A: Coming to Israel cuts you bare. That's the inner essence of the landscape. And that's what Israel did to my work: it cut the poems back to a naked speaking. Israel also freed me in a way from the need to write about the Holocaust. I don't have to carry it personally anymore; the whole country is carrying it. In Australia, I felt I was always screaming: 'People, don't you understand? Look what happened!' They suspect you're a propagandist for even talking about the Holocaust. But in Israel, you can take it for granted that people will understand the context you're working in. As a Jewish poet, you can get to essence directly.

Q: Much of your poetry since coming to Israel is about rootedness, the struggle to become re-planted in Israeli soil.
A: Everything is your's here, the snowstorms, the problems; every thing is part of your own soul. I find it difficult even to take a political stand, because each ideological position resonates and expresses an aspect of my Jewish psyche. Left, right—every voice is speaking a certain truth, expressing a different idea or era of Jewish history. Politics isn't abstract here: it is the meaning of your own life that's being debated. What happened to me in these last ten years is that I've become a Jew. By speaking as an Israeli Jew, you have much more to say to the world than you do as a Diaspora Jew. It has a greater truth, a greater authenticity. You come closer to a dialogue with the nations because you're speaking from your own knowledge instead of constantly translating.

You are an elder of your nation, sitting with the elders of the earth—African, Chinese, Indian—holding your people's ancient wisdom.

Q: Kabbalistic concepts and imagery—our ancient wisdom—suffuse *Desire for White* and of course *Kabbalah and Consciousness*. How did your interest in Kabbalah develop?
A: I formed a connection with a Kabbalist, a Chabad hasid, Rabbi Yitzchak Ginsburgh. We got together regularly and talked. *Kabbalah and Consciousness* came out of those sessions. It's an account of a modern person in intimate confrontational discussion with a Kabbalist—I learned Kabbalah and Hasidism in a direct way. We used my poems, my own experience, as a kind of Mishna, a text around which to argue. I found that the Jewish tradition understood my soul better than I did. I felt my brothers calling to me, teaching me, and especially, recognizing me.

Q: In *Desire for White*, one senses that you are writing about the mystical encounter from personal experience.
A: The central reality of *Desire for White* is that of a person who's experienced the unity of existence. The basic principle of Kabbalah is the interconnectedness of life. The Sh'ma prayer: Adonai Ehad, God is one. *Desire for White* starts with the assumption of that reality. Everything is light. That is the messianic call: go back to God, end this existence, this game. We have no choice but to return to You.

Q: Stanley Moss took the already-published *Purple Adam* and combined it with *Desire for White* into a single book. The *Purple Adam* poems are very personal—farm, family, children, your encounter with the Holocaust. But *Desire for White* seems transpersonal. How does that juxtaposition work for you?
A: *Desire for White* is very spare, a direct conversation with Ein Soff, the Infinite. The humanity of *Purple Adam* forms the grounding experience—the human credentials-from which that conversation can take place. The experience of the land and the children and the holocaust and my previous existentialism—I bring all that in my confrontation with the Infinite. The two

210

groups of poems share the same movement—from hester panim, the hiddenness of God, to tikkun, the revelation of God's presence in the world. The first section of *Purple Adam* deals with the holocaust and the Tasmanian genocide and death in nature. Then the poems move to a celebration of my son Adam's birth, of being a father, of finding one's place. That same movement—from God's hiddenness to celebration of life—occurs in *Desire for White*, only at a higher turn of the spiral. The first part of the work expresses the pain of humanity's distance from God, of its inability to hold the light, to reveal God's existence: we just can't do it without You. Then it moves into a cycle of love poems to Susan, an echo of the Song of Songs. The last lines of *Desire for White*, asking God to "kiss us who miss you," isn't coming out of suffering but from a deeper longing. It's coming out of the fertile life I share with Susan.

Q: How does your writing process work?
A: A poem usually begins with an image or an idea that starts to resonate, to become compulsive. I can feel when something wants to come out. I wait for it. I let it sit until it more or less forces itself out. Then I rewrite a lot—it doesn't emerge as a full poem. I can do twenty or a hundred drafts. Purifying the poem. My drafts can fill a car (*laughter*). It's like a birth. Even after birth, the poem is full of blood, ego, cliche. The poem has to be stripped away, until I discover its essence. *Desire for White* was an exception. It took only about a month or two to write. For me, that's as if it came out fully formed (*laughter*).

Q: And yet *Desire for White* is your most complex work. How did it develop?
A: I was walking in the desert and this form, this voice came out. Each line undercutting the one above it. Like a waterfall. Most of *Desire for White* was written in the desert. The desert doesn't let you hold any idea very long. It strips essence from essence, and that's how the poem moves. You get to an idea, then it strips away—into another revelation, another revelation. The desert is a very good critic. Whatever I write, I test out by reading in the desert. If it works for me there, I know it's ok.

211

Q: But there's an exuberance in *Desire for White*, despite the spareness, even severity of its style.

A: To write a poem that is critical or bitter just doesn't seem worthwhile to me. Why bother? The Jewish attitude is to sing. Not out of a combative national pride. Just to sing our own inner song.

Q: How do you reconcile that song with your line about the Holocaust in *Purple Adam*: 'Why is it that every moment we are awake we do not weep?'

A: That's exactly the point. The Jewish way is to know the world, to deny nothing—holding the Holocaust, holding the anger and the bitterness—and sing. Both *Desire for White* and *Kabbalah and Consciousness* try to express the inner life—the inner song—of Jewish mysticism. I wanted to say: Despite everything, the Jewish people is alive. Despite our brokenness, we're still able to sing. What drew me to Judaism was the Jewish ability to know the world without illusions and still praise God. The Jews, the most wounded people, always find ways to praise life, to praise, to praise, to praise. What is the Kaddish? A song of praise to God. That's been the driving principle of my life: to sing and praise and not die in some empty bitterness or regret. I'd like to be one poet singing one version of our song. If I could write one Psalm, one song of praise that would stay with the Jewish people, it would be enough.

Yossi Klein Halevi